CAST YOUR BREAD UPON THE WATERS

Sister Schubert
CAST YOUR BREAD UPON THE WATERS
- Recipes for Success, Cooking & Living -

{the idea boutique}®

SECOND EDITION

Copyright © 2010 by CECA Enterprises, LLC

Photography © 2010 by Paul Poplis, Vickie Popwell, Romona Robbins
and
Cornerstone Marketing & Advertising, Inc.; by Jessie Shepard and John Hollerand.
All rights reserved.

{the idea boutique}®

Cornerstone Marketing & Advertising, Inc., 114 Logan Lane, Suite 4, Grayton Beach, FL 32459
E-mail: Info@TheIdeaBoutique.com
Author: Patricia "Sister" Schubert Barnes
Foreword: Chrissie Schubert Duffy
Recipe Production Manager & Editor: Charlotte H. Wood
Editor: Lisa M. Burwell
Managing Editor: Laurie A. Crowley
Copy Editor: Margaret Stevenson
Indexer: Crystal Hamon
Production Manager: Gerald F. Burwell
VP of Web Design: R.M. Brown
Art Direction & Design: Eric Shepard
Photographers: Paul Poplis, Vickie Popwell, Jessie Shepard, John Hollerand, and Romona Robbins
Food Stylist: Sharon Reiss

Library of Congress Control Number: 2010929568
ISBN-13: 978-0-615-37658-5
www.CastYourBreadUponTheWaters.com

Sister Schubert's is a registered trademark of Sister Schubert's Homemade Rolls, Inc. and is used under license. This work is subject to copyright. All rights reserved. Except for in a review, the reproduction or utilization of this work in any form or by any electronic, mechanical, or other means, now known or hereafter invented, including xerography, photocopying, and recording, and any information storage and retrieval system, is forbidden without permission of the publisher.

PRINTED WITH PRIDE IN THE UNITED STATES OF AMERICA

DEDICATION

I dedicate this cookbook to my grandmother, Leona Henderson Wood, affectionately known to my family as "Gommey," who shared with me her love of baking bread, managing a family and a business, and most importantly, doing it all with God's help. Her recipe for *Everlasting Rolls* is the seed which started Sister Schubert's Homemade Rolls, but her legacy is felt far beyond the kitchen. Her children, grandchildren, and great-grandchildren have been blessed by her spiritual guidance, her wisdom, and her love.

Indeed, this book is for all grandmothers who teach their children and grandchildren by their own example of unyielding love and unwavering inspiration.

"Gommey" loved this verse from the Bible, and lived it:

"Let the words of my mouth and the meditation of my heart be acceptable in thy sight, O LORD, my strength and my redeemer."
—Psalm 19:14 (KJV)

"Cast your bread upon the waters, for after many days you will find it again."
—Ecclesiastes 11:1 (NIV)

And, I extend my heartfelt thanks to my sister Charlotte, who has been an invaluable source and inspiration for me to do this book. Without her support and guidance, I would not have been able to accomplish the publication of this, which has been my heart's desire and means so much to me.

TABLE OF CONTENTS

Foreword 8

Introduction 9

Chapter 1 – Success 10

Chapter 2 – Cooking 20

Homemade Rolls 22

Butters 37

Breakfast & Brunch 38

Main Dishes 62

Breads 74

The Bread of Life 108

Sides & Veggies 116

Desserts & Beverages 126

Holiday Favorites 138

Chapter 3 – Living 162

Index 176

FOREWORD

By Chrissie Schubert Duffy

Growing up in a family with an entrepreneurial spirit can do one of two things to a person. Either the individual vows never to undertake the enormous task of running his or her own business, or he or she embraces the challenge and commits to the uncertainty of success. Thanks to my mother, I chose the latter. I think there are times (mostly at the end of an extremely long day) when I question whether I made the right choice!

I watched, firsthand, as my mother, Patricia "Sister" Schubert Barnes, started baking rolls at home. I remember wearing a lace apron as I helped to deliver her delicious rolls to the local market. I watched as she grew the business from the sun porch to a factory. She was bold, gracious, determined, and tireless. Her unwavering faith in God and in herself set an example for her children that could not be taught in any business school. We learned by example.

I am fortunate, as a business owner, that I can call my mom for advice or if I just need to talk to someone who has "been there." I encourage you not only to try my mom's recipes but also to read her inspirational words in this cookbook. She has remarkable insight into life's challenges and triumphs, and with her optimistic flair, she will inspire you to embrace life!

INTRODUCTION

I have always believed that each of us has dreams and desires, and talents waiting to be uncovered. They start with a tiny seed: a seed that we "cast" or plant, so that it can take root and grow. A seed must be cultivated with patience and love, and through faith it will take root and prosper. We cannot see what is taking place underground, yet we anticipate the arrival of that first bud, the spirit of the flower. For each of us, every seed we sow has great potential, but it is up to us to feed our dreams, nurture our ideas, and have faith that our talent will blossom. A seed, however, is just a seed, without hard work and care.

I did not wake up one day and decide that I wanted to be the head of a very successful company, but each step along the path from my kitchen table to the boardroom at Sister Schubert's Homemade Rolls helped to prepare me for the next step. I tended each idea, each seed, with careful attention and with faith, and eventually they grew into a company that I am proud of, and I am grateful that it carries my name. I am still learning and growing, and I believe every day brings another opportunity to use the gifts that God gave us: faith, hope, and love. Cast Your Bread Upon the Waters is not only a cookbook but also a way to share my love of family, faith, and of course, cooking. Enjoy!

CHAPTER 1 SUCCESS

SISTER & CHARLOTTE

GREAT BEGINNINGS

For as long as I can remember, I have loved cooking, and thankfully, the wonderful cooks in my family were only too glad to share their experience and love of good food with me. My mother taught me how to bake the lightest Whipped Cream Pound Cake with sweet, silky Rum Sauce, and savory Cheese Straws. From our cook, Mary Stark (whom we children called "Mamie"), I learned to make perfect biscuits and cornbreads and the best fried chicken in Alabama. And "Gommey" (my grandmother Wood) showed me how to make her best "receipts," tried-and-true recipes handed down from her mother and grandmother: Southern favorites like Fly-off-the-Plate Pancakes, Banana Bread, and her buttery, light-as-a-feather Parker House–style rolls, which she called *Everlasting Rolls*. She showed me how to judge the water temperature by touch so that the yeast bloomed just right; how to handle the warm, sticky dough gently; and where to place the tea-towel-covered bowl of dough for the best rising.

In the beginning, I baked Gommey's *Everlasting Rolls* for my family. Then, I made a brief foray into catering and baked them for parties; I realized that I enjoyed feeding people, not just my own family, but others as well. Then for Christmas of 1986, my church held a frozen food fair. Participants listed their specialty dishes, and the church secretary took orders for delivery during the holidays, with the proceeds going to charity. I tested a few batches of rolls in the freezer, and discovered that they held up very well, and baked true to form after thawing. That year, I received orders for eighty pans of "Sister's Rolls" and managed to fill them by Christmas Eve. The next year, there were two hundred orders, and once again, with help from willing family members, we delivered the rolls. But the following year, when the church secretary called to say she had stopped taking orders at three hundred pans, I knew I had something special. With help from neighbors, family, and friends, we managed to get all of the rolls delivered, and even had a pan for our own Christmas dinner.

I gathered flour, foil pans, plastic freezer bags, and stick-on labels from the grocery store and started baking. I took a pan of rolls to Mrs. Ingram at Ingram's Curb Market in Troy, Alabama, who ordered a dozen pans on a trial basis. Armed with white lacy aprons and silver trays, my daughters, Charlotte and Chrissie, and I handed out samples at Ingram's, and Sister Schubert's Homemade Rolls was born. The hand-typed labels often fell off in the freezer, and the rolls were delivered in my old station wagon, but the orders kept coming. Soon I outgrew my kitchen at home and took the first of many steps along the path to Sister Schubert's today. But the best part is that my rolls are made the same way today as they were made in the beginning—using pure, simple ingredients and no preservatives, just the same as Gommey made them. It's a pleasure to share them with you, along with all the other Sister Schubert's Homemade Rolls and cornbread.

Pictured above (left to right):
Charlotte, Sister, and younger sister, Lesa

THE BREAD AND BUTTER OF THE BUSINESS

Everlasting Rolls

It is so fitting that Gommey called her Parker House–style rolls *Everlasting Rolls*, because the blessings that have flowed from her recipe will surely last a lifetime. She taught me how to bake, but she also taught me to appreciate the time spent with others while baking. I cherished my time in the kitchen with her. Somehow the conversations we had there flowed freely from one topic to the next. I never wanted the rolls to be done because that would mean our special time would be over. But then she would surprise me with a glass of iced tea and a fresh-from-the-oven treat, and we would sit at the kitchen table and continue chatting.

On my twenty-first birthday, Gommey gave me her favorite cookbook, complete with personal tips and notes in her handwriting. I will always be grateful for her gift. I know now, by sharing her love of baking, she planted a seed. She saw something in me that she knew would somehow bless others. That seed, planted with love, has firmly taken root and has blossomed into a spiritual blessing that has touched many lives around the world. I believe, as long as we are good stewards of God's gifts, they will be *everlasting*.

"As the rain and the snow come down from heaven, and do not return to it without watering the earth and making it bud and flourish, so that it yields seed for the sower and bread for the eater, so is my word that goes out of my mouth: It will not return to me empty, but will accomplish what I desire and achieve the purpose for which I sent it."

—Isaiah 55:10

Pictured top left:
Leona "Gommey" Henderson Wood

EVERLASTING ROLLS
Page 26

STEPPING OUT IN FAITH

"Do not despise these small beginnings, for the Lord rejoices to see the work begin..."
—Zechariah 4:10

Ribbon cutting for Luverne bakery, 1994

Sister Schubert's Homemade Rolls was founded in Troy, Alabama in 1991. It took a lot of courage and faith to step out of my kitchen and start the next chapter of my life—as an *entrepreneur*. As with every important decision in my life, I prayed about it and asked God to guide me. I can say with all honesty that I knew this was what I should be doing. I did not know why or where it would lead me, but I felt confident in my decision. The early years were exciting, difficult, scary, and exhausting, but we were all having a wonderful time. There is nothing more gratifying than growing an idea into a reality. I want to emphasize that I did not do this all on my own; just because my name is on the product does not mean I was a one-woman show. My family was truly inspirational and supportive, and they were my initial workforce. Trusted friends became employees, and their energy and enthusiasm kept me going. Even though I had a great product, there was no guarantee it would be a success. But I believe in *hard work*, faith in yourself, *hard work*, faith in the product, *hard work*, faith in your employees, *hard work*—well, I think you get the point. Success does not happen overnight, but with hard work and faith, it will happen.

In the beginning, Sister Schubert's Homemade Rolls really were homemade—in my home. I went to Sears and bought the largest double residential oven they had. It was too big to fit in my kitchen, so I set it up on the sun porch. My mother gave me a chest freezer as a gift, which we placed next to the oven. We made the dough in my little Sunbeam mixer and cut out the rolls by hand. The sun porch became a mini-bakery, complete with a plastic flap door to keep the humidity and heat in the room correctly balanced. Our dining room table served as a cooling and packaging area.

At first, I called on small groceries in Montgomery, Dothan, and Birmingham, Alabama. If a grocer agreed to sell my rolls, then the girls and I set up in the store and handed out samples. I knew that if I could get people to taste my rolls, they would buy them.

After operating out of my home for almost a year, I decided to take a giant step by setting up a commercial bakery. In 1992, I found a wholesale supplier for ingredients and

packaging and bought some used commercial ovens and a little 20-quart commercial mixer. I say "little" now, but it looked like a monster to me the first time I saw it. My father had a furniture warehouse in downtown Troy, and we set up our bakery in 1,000 square feet there. Within six months, we had to move the furniture out and take over the whole warehouse.

What's next? A question we all ask ourselves routinely…the project is well begun, but what happens now? I have often said that the "next step" is the hardest step! For me, the next step seemed to happen on a daily basis, because although I was confident in my ability to bake bread, I had to learn about the *business* of baking bread. First, I needed to translate Gommey's recipe for four pans of rolls into hundreds, and then thousands of pans, while ensuring that the taste, texture, and quality remained the same. And then we had to consider the logistics of packaging, marketing, purchasing, and plant management—all steps along my path. Thinking back to those hectic days when we faced new challenges every week, I cannot imagine how we got it all done.

It did not take long before I no longer could call on new markets, supervise production, and manage delivery all by myself. I turned to George Barnes, a food broker. He expanded our distribution from a few local groceries to major grocery chains throughout the South. He became the other half of the Sister Schubert management team and my own better half when we were married in 1995.

People kept talking about our rolls, and pretty soon orders were outpacing production at our little bakery. In 1994, we opened a new, state-of-the-art facility in Luverne, Alabama. It was a huge risk, but I saw it as an affirmation of my faith and my vision for the company. With 25,000 square feet, I thought the Luverne bakery provided all the space we needed. But by 1998, we had completed two expansions, and with a total of 80,000 square feet, we were making more than one million rolls per day.

Pictured top right:
Interior of Sister's first bakery in Troy, Alabama

RECOGNIZE AN OPPORTUNITY

By that time, my rolls had attracted the attention of several large corporations, who approached me about buying the company. I was not interested at first, but eventually, in 2000, we decided to sell our stock to Lancaster Colony Corporation, a consumer goods company focusing on specialty foods, based in Columbus, Ohio. We did it for two reasons: first, they had the resources to propel Sister Schubert to national brand status. But more importantly, they had a history of purchasing family-run companies and then keeping the families on board to run the company.

This was of utmost importance to us and should be to anyone who has an original idea or product. Sometimes you may be enticed by the money to sell and let someone else run the business; but when your name is on the product, you have an obligation to ensure its integrity. Today, Sister Schubert's Homemade Rolls, Inc. is part of Lancaster Colony's specialty foods division.

George and I are still actively involved with the company: I am Founder and Vice President of Product Development and Manufacturing, and George is Vice President of Operations. With the opening of our new 105,000-square-foot facility in Horse Cave, Kentucky, we could not feel more blessed. Sister Schubert's Homemade Rolls continues to grow. We add new products and expand into a larger geographic region each year, and you can now buy our rolls all across the United States.

Through the years, we have stayed true to our roots. Our rolls have the same homebaked quality and taste as my grandmother's. We use simple, wholesome ingredients like fresh milk, butter, and whole eggs—never any preservatives! And every single roll is still placed in the pan by hand. Never skimp on the quality of the ingredients. This true statement is the heart of my business, and it applies to everything, not just the flour, sugar, butter, and salt. I encourage you to always use the best quality ingredients available to you. Get friendly with the butcher at your local grocery store; he's your source for great meats. You do not have to buy prepackaged meat when he and his staff are happy to cut your request to order at no extra cost. Visit your local farmers' market when vegetables and fruits are in season. You'll get the freshest, ripest produce at reasonable prices and support your local farmers at the same time. It's a win-win concept! The flavor of fresh herbs is far superior to the dried variety, and you can use leftovers for garnish. I use real butter at the bakery and at home, but of course, you must make an adjustment if you have dietary restrictions. I have not specified brand names for ingredients in these recipes; rather, I suggest you use "premium" products. My great-aunt Charlotte, a well-known epicurean in Houston, Texas, once told me, "The finest company that ever put their feet under my table is my family." I agree; don't you?

Pictured above:
Production floor of Troy bakery

ENCOURAGE TEAMWORK

"A generous man will himself be blessed, for he shares his food with the poor."
—Proverbs 22:9

In the early days, the bakery ran full production from Monday through Saturday, leaving Sundays for family and faith. When orders began to regularly outpace production, I realized that I would have to ask my staff to work on Sundays. I looked at my co-workers, my wonderful bakery team: women (and a few brave men) who had been by my side on the journey from tiny to tremendous. I assured them that I would be there on alternating Sundays; I praised them for their dedication and hard work . . . and I held my breath. Would they stay? They did, and on the first of many Sundays at the bakery, with flour swirling around us, we sang the beautiful old spirituals—one hundred voices raised in praise and thanksgiving. Those rolls were surely blessed!

I am grateful for those loyal employees and thank them for helping me continue my *purpose* in life. I am able to give back in so many different ways now, and that never would have happened without their devoted spirit. *Never underestimate the impact that others have on your success.*

I have talked with many successful men and women. One common theme I've heard time and again is *purpose*. Each one of these people believes that what they are doing has a greater purpose than just earning money for personal gain. When that theory was the dominant motivator, they actually earned more money or were more successful towards their goal, which leads me to believe that *what you do can earn you money, but why you do it can earn you so much more!*

Whether you desire to be a successful entrepreneur, mother, wife and homemaker, or best friend, the same principles apply. Your purpose or intent must be pure. Success is measured in so many ways; it is up to each of us to find our purpose in life, so that God can use us to bless others.

CHAPTER 2 COOKING

EVERLASTING ROLLS
Page 26

1

HOMEMADE ROLLS

Making homemade rolls from scratch may seem like a daunting task, but remember, women have been baking their own bread since the beginning of time. How hard can it be? Well, I joke here to make a point. Most of us more "mature" people never thought we would master the computer, but we did (with the help of our children). So, you can certainly try your hand at making homemade rolls, and maybe even learn a skill to pass down to your children and grandchildren. I have included tips on baking with yeast and creative variations of rolls for you to try. Enjoy!

BAKING WITH YEAST

The aroma and flavor of freshly baked yeast bread has enriched lives for centuries, and although I understand how it works, I still marvel at the magic in the kneading and rising of the dough, the magic in the fragrant scent of warm bread coming out of my oven, and the magic in savoring the warm crusty loaf. In case you need a refresher course on baking with yeast, here are some tried-and-true tips:

Yeast is a living organism, and the temperature of liquids is very important to success with yeast bread. Invest in a good candy thermometer, and use it!

Check the date on your yeast before you begin. If you think that the yeast may not be viable, proof to be sure. Add 1 tablespoon sugar to ½ cup warm water (100°F); stir until dissolved. Stir in 1 package active dry yeast, and let stand for 8 to 10 minutes. The yeast should form a creamy foam on the surface of the water, and you may proceed with your recipe. (Remember to adjust sugar and water amounts to accommodate the proof.)

Do not use "bread" flour unless specified by the recipe. I use all-purpose flour for home baking, so nearly all of these recipes call for all-purpose flour.

Measure ingredients with the correct measuring cups. For flour, use a straight edged measuring cup with measurements marked to the rim. Place the cup on a paper plate, and spoon flour into the cup, allowing it to spill over the edges. Level with the back of a knife, and do not lose count! For liquids, use a spouted measuring cup and a spatula to release all of the ingredient you are measuring. Measuring spoons should be leveled unless the directions call for "heaping."

Bread baking is an inexact art; factors like humidity and water quality figure into the equation. You may need a little more (or less) flour for certain recipes. Go with my description of how the dough should feel, and if you think it needs a little more flour, you're probably right!

When a warm liquid mixture is added to a flour mixture that includes dry yeast, extra beating with the mixer helps the yeast dissolve completely.

Don't panic if you have to leave your yeast dough for a few moments. Yeast dough can rest, covered, on a work surface for up to

30 minutes, or it can be refrigerated for one to two hours, unless otherwise directed. Remember to allow it to return to room temperature before continuing your recipe.

"A warm place"…you will see this direction over and over again. Find a spot with no drafts, about 85°F is best, but any warm room will do. Your laundry room is usually ideal, especially with the dryer running to supply extra humidity and the door closed to prevent drafts.

As an alternative, the oven is a perfect draft-free, temperature-controlled environment for dough to rise. Place the dough on the middle rack and a pan of hot water on the bottom rack. Close the oven door, and allow the yeast to go to work.

Rising times are approximate, and you should gauge the quantity of your dough rather than the time it has risen. Usually, recipes call for the dough to "double" in bulk, so make a mental note of the size when you begin the rise.

A tea towel is simply a cotton dish towel wet and thoroughly wrung out to provide a moisture boost to your dough while it rises. Do not substitute paper towels, as they will stick to the dough when dry.

Preheat the oven before you begin your final preparation, and the oven will be ready when you are. During the first 10 to 15 minutes of baking, heat causes the dough to expand quickly, form the crust, and give shape to the loaf. If the oven is not preheated, the dough may over-rise before the crust is formed, resulting in a misshapen loaf.

Bake on the center rack of the oven unless the recipe directs otherwise.

If yeast breads start to over-brown before they are done, shield the loaves with aluminum foil for the remainder of the baking time.

Remove breads and rolls from the pans immediately after baking unless otherwise directed. Steam condensation can cause soggy crusts.

Use a serrated knife to slice bread neatly with less loss of crumb.

EVERLASTING ROLLS

EVERLASTING ROLLS

Parker House–Style Rolls

Gommey taught me to bake bread with these rolls. In her version of the recipe, ingredients were listed in "heaping" pints and "scant" quarts instead of cups. Also, she called for the dough to be "taken up" and for the baking to be done in a "quick" oven. It was an adventure to translate everything for today's baker. This is my favorite bread in the world, and I know that you will love it as I do.

EVERLASTING ROLLS
Parker House–Style Rolls

1 package active dry yeast

1½ cups warm water (105°F to 115°F)

5 cups sifted all-purpose flour, divided

½ cup sugar

1½ teaspoons salt

½ cup shortening, melted (cooled to 105°F to 115°F)

2 large eggs, lightly beaten

½ cup butter, melted

1¼ cups all-purpose flour

Combine yeast and warm water in a 2-cup liquid measuring cup; let stand 5 minutes.

Combine 4 cups sifted flour, sugar, and salt in a large bowl. Stir in yeast mixture and shortening. Add eggs and remaining 1 cup sifted flour; stir vigorously until well blended. (Dough will be soft and sticky.) Brush or lightly rub dough with some of the melted butter. Cover loosely with a damp tea towel; let rise in a warm place (85°F), free from drafts, for 1½ hours or until doubled in bulk.

Grease four (8-inch) round foil cake pans; set aside.

Sift ¾ cup flour in a thick layer evenly over work surface; turn dough out onto floured surface. (Dough will be soft.) Sift ½ cup flour evenly over dough. Roll dough to ½-inch thickness; brush off excess flour.

Cut out dough using a floured 2-inch biscuit cutter. Pull each round into an oval, approximately 2½ inches long. Dip one side of oval into melted butter. Fold oval in half with buttered side facing out. (Floured side will form the famous Parker House pocket.)

For each pan, place the folds of 10 rolls against side of prepared pan, pressing center fronts of rolls together gently to seal. Place 5 rolls in inner circle, and 1 roll in center, for a total of 16 rolls per pan. Cover loosely with a damp tea towel, and let rise in a warm place, free from drafts, for 1 hour or until doubled in bulk.

Preheat oven to 400°F.

Bake rolls, uncovered, for 12 to 15 minutes or until lightly browned.

Yield: 64 rolls

WHOLE WHEAT ROLLS

Whole Wheat Variation:

Substitute 2 cups whole wheat flour and 3 cups all-purpose flour for the 5 cups all-purpose flour listed above. Instead of plain melted butter for dipping the rolls, use ½ cup melted butter mixed with 2 tablespoons honey. Bake as directed for *Everlasting Rolls*.

If you are baking rolls for your freezer, allow the pans to completely cool on wire racks, then slide each pan into a large zipper bag and freeze. Do not stack pans until completely frozen. To reheat, allow rolls to thaw completely and heat at 350°F for 10 minutes.

Sister says:

These are my favorite rolls, and they are yours to bake and enjoy. The secret to the light-as-a-feather texture of these rolls: Don't knead the dough!

Baking yeast bread is not time consuming, but the rising times require your attention. Plan to be at home for a span of 4 hours. The recipe makes 4 pans: one for dinner, two for the freezer and one to share with a friend who will be amazed at your skill in the kitchen!

Where's the best place in your home for the dough to rise? It's your laundry room. Wash a load of towels and put them into the dryer. Cover the top of the dryer with a clean towel and place your dough on top. Be sure to cover the dough loosely with a damp tea towel. Turn on the dryer and close the laundry room door. The heat and humidity create a good environment for yeast activation and your laundry will serve two purposes.

Relax and enjoy the heavenly aroma of freshly baked yeast rolls!

ORANGE ROLLS

ORANGE ROLLS

2 cups sugar

1 cup butter, melted

¾ cup coarsely grated orange rind (5 oranges)

1 recipe *Everlasting Rolls* dough (page 28)

1½ cups all-purpose flour, divided

½ cup butter, melted

2½ cups powdered sugar, sifted

¼ cup fresh orange juice

½ cup coarsely grated orange rind (3 oranges)

Combine first 3 ingredients; set aside. Grease four (8-inch) round cake pans; set aside.

After *Everlasting Rolls* dough has risen per directions, sift ½ cup flour in a thick layer evenly over work surface. Turn half of dough out onto floured surface. (Dough will be very soft.) Set remaining half of dough aside.

Sift ¼ cup flour evenly over dough. Roll dough into a 30 x 20-inch rectangle. Spread half of orange rind mixture over dough. Starting at the short side, roll up dough jelly-roll fashion just to the center of the rectangle; cut dough along side of roll to release it. Roll up remaining half of rectangle in the same fashion. Set rolls of dough aside. Repeat procedure using remaining ¾ cup flour, dough, and orange rind mixture.

Cut each roll of dough into 16 (1¼-inch-thick) slices. Place 16 slices, cut sides down, in each prepared pan, leaving ¼-inch space between slices. Brush slices with ½ cup melted butter. Let rise, uncovered, in a warm place (85°F), free from drafts, for 1 hour or until doubled in bulk.

Preheat oven to 375°F.

Bake rolls, uncovered, for 15 to 18 minutes or until lightly browned. Cool slightly in pans on wire racks. Combine powdered sugar, orange juice, and ½ cup orange rind, drizzle over warm rolls.

Yield: 64 rolls

Blueberry Cream Cheese Variation:

Prepare basic rolls as directed. Cream cheese filling: Combine 1 pound powdered sugar with 8 ounces softened cream cheese, beating until smooth. Wash and stem 2 pints blueberries; dry on paper towels. Spread filling mixture as directed above; sprinkle with blueberries. Continue recipe as directed. Icing for Blueberry Rolls is the same as for Cinnamon Rolls.

Sister says:

Orange Rolls are my mother's favorites, and the key ingredient is fresh oranges. The aroma of yeast bread and orange zest is hard to beat! At home, I use a citrus zester to get the rich oily rind just below the surface of the orange, leaving the pithy white membrane intact.

CINNAMON ROLLS

1 cup sugar

1 cup butter, melted

½ cup ground cinnamon

1 recipe *Everlasting Rolls* dough (page 28)

1½ cups all-purpose flour, divided

½ cup butter, melted

2½ cups sifted powdered sugar

¼ cup milk

1 teaspoon vanilla extract

Combine first 3 ingredients; set aside. Grease four (8-inch) round cake pans; set aside.

After *Everlasting Rolls* dough has risen per directions, sift ½ cup flour in a thick layer evenly over work surface. Turn half of dough out onto floured surface. (Dough will be very soft.) Set remaining half of dough aside.

Sift ¼ cup flour evenly over dough. Roll dough into a 30 x 20-inch rectangle. Spread half of cinnamon mixture over dough. Starting at the short side, roll up dough jelly-roll fashion just to the center of the rectangle; cut dough along side of roll to release it. Roll up remaining half of rectangle in the same fashion. Set rolls of dough aside. Repeat procedure using remaining ¾ cup flour, dough, and cinnamon mixture.

Cut each roll of dough into 16 (1¼-inch-thick) slices. Place 16 slices, cut sides down, in each prepared pan, leaving ¼-inch space between slices. Brush slices with ½ cup melted butter. Let rise, uncovered, in a warm place (85°F), free from drafts, for 1 hour or until doubled in bulk.

Preheat oven to 375°F.

Bake rolls, uncovered, for 15 to 18 minutes or until lightly browned. Cool slightly in pans on wire racks.

Combine powdered sugar, milk, and vanilla, stirring until smooth; drizzle over warm rolls.

Yield: 64 rolls

Sister says: *If you like raisins or pecans in your cinnamon rolls, sprinkle them over the cinnamon mixture before rolling up and slicing the rolls. You will need ½ cup per rectangle, or 2 cups total. Enjoy!*

SAUSAGE ROLLS

Place sausages in a single layer in a shallow pan. Bake at 350°F for 20 minutes. To avoid greasy rolls, pat cooked sausages dry on paper towels.

To assemble, fold the buttered cut-out dough for *Everlasting Rolls* around the cooked sausages before placing rolls in the prepared pans. Continue preparing rolls as directed in *Everlasting Rolls* recipe (page 28).

Yield: 64 rolls

64 smoked cocktail sausages

1 recipe *Everlasting Rolls* dough (page 28)

CHEDDAR ROLLS

Slice cheese crosswise into 16 strips; slice strips in half. Open each roll, and place 1 cheese piece in center; close rolls. Return rolls to pans; cover loosely with aluminum foil.

Bake at 350°F for 10 minutes or until cheese is melted. Serve warm.

Yield: 32 rolls

1 (8-ounce) package extra-sharp cheddar cheese

2 pans baked Sister Schubert's Parker House Rolls or Sourdough Rolls

MEDITERRANEAN ROLLS

8 ounces crumbled feta cheese

⅓ cup premium mayonnaise

¼ cup sun-dried tomatoes in oil, chopped

2 teaspoons chopped fresh basil or ¾ teaspoon dried basil

½ teaspoon black pepper

2 pans baked Sister Schubert's Parker House Rolls or Sourdough Rolls

Combine first 5 ingredients. Open each roll, and spread each with about 1 teaspoon cheese mixture; close rolls. Return rolls to pans; cover loosely with aluminum foil.

Bake at 350°F for 10 minutes or until thoroughly heated. Serve warm.

Yield: 32 rolls

TURKEY ROLLS

2 pans baked Sister Schubert's Parker House Rolls or Sourdough Rolls

1 (8-ounce) jar orange marmalade

1 pound cooked turkey, thinly sliced

Open each roll, and spread each with 1½ teaspoons orange marmalade. Place a slice of turkey over marmalade; close rolls. Return rolls to pans; cover loosely with aluminum foil.

Bake at 350°F for 15 to 20 minutes or until thoroughly heated. Serve warm.

Yield: 32 rolls

MEDITERRANEAN ROLLS

TOASTED ROLL BITES

1 pan Sister Schubert's Parker House Rolls, thawed

Butter, softened to room temperature

Preheat oven to 425°F. Move oven rack to top position.

Line a rimmed baking sheet with parchment paper.

Remove rolls from pan and separate. Slice each roll in half and spread with butter. Place roll bites on prepared pan and bake until lightly browned around edges.

Yield: 32 bites

Sister says: This is my favorite way to use leftover rolls. For a sweet treat, add a generous sprinkle of cinnamon sugar. I promise there will be no leftovers!

HERB BUTTER

Combine all ingredients. Gently brush butter mixture over tops of Sister Schubert's Parker House Rolls or Sourdough Rolls just before baking.

Yield: 1 cup

1 cup butter, softened

1 tablespoon sesame seeds

1 teaspoon celery seeds

1 teaspoon poppy seeds

⅛ teaspoon garlic powder

MAYTAG BLUE CHEESE BUTTER

Combine butter and cheese, stirring until well blended. Cover tightly and store in the refrigerator.

½ cup butter, softened

2 tablespoons crumbled Maytag Blue Cheese

Sister says: This tangy butter is perfect with cornbread. Maytag Blue Cheese is my longtime favorite, and an all-American product. I hope you like it too!

HONEY BUTTER

Combine butter and honey, stirring until well blended. Gently brush butter mixture over Whole Wheat Rolls before baking.

Yield: ½ cup

½ cup butter, softened

2 tablespoons honey

STRAWBERRIES & CREAM CREPES
Page 45

2

BREAKFAST & BRUNCH

Preparations for an elegant formal dinner can start weeks in advance. Making the guest list, writing out the invitations, planning the menu, polishing the silver, ironing the tablecloths, and washing the formal china are only a few of the details on my checklist. While I thoroughly enjoy all that goes into hosting a formal occasion, I realize that not many busy working moms have the time for this. However, I do not believe that we should put off having friends and family over for a meal because we feel we do not have time for labor-intensive preparations.

That is why I love brunch. Brunch is informal, yet it has an eclectic charm that allows us to follow the ebb and flow of the day. A casual table setting paired with flowers from the yard can be put together at a moment's notice. The charm and style you provide will put your guests at ease. Whether served indoors or out, brunch can be prepared in advance so that you can spend time with your guests and enjoy the meal, without being tied to the kitchen. After all, while the food is important, it's the interaction with others that truly feeds the soul.

The following recipes offer something for everyone, from variations on my delicious rolls to Crepes 4 Ways (pages 40–45) and Cheesy Shrimp and Grits (page 49). These are my own family favorites as well as classic Southern recipes. With a little preparation, your brunch will be almost effortless.

CREPES FOUR WAYS
Crepe Batter

8 eggs

½ teaspoon salt

4 cups all-purpose flour

4 cups whole milk

7 tablespoons butter, melted

Butter for the pan

Using a large mixing bowl, beat eggs with salt until frothy. Add flour gradually, alternating flour and milk; beat on medium speed until smooth. With mixer on low speed, add melted butter, beating until well combined. Cover tightly and refrigerate for 3 to 4 hours or overnight.

Before cooking, allow batter to return to room temperature and skim bubbles from surface.

Heat a non-stick crepe pan or seasoned skillet until a few drops of water dance, wipe dry and brush lightly with melted butter. Pour ¼ cup batter into center of crepe pan and swirl to coat surface. Cook over medium heat for 30 to 40 seconds. (The bottom of the crepe will be lightly browned.) Shake or jerk the pan to dislodge the crepe and flip to complete cooking. (You can use your fingers or a spatula to turn!) Cook only 15 seconds more and remove crepe to wire rack to cool.

Yield: 50 to 60 crepes

Sister says: *Cooked, cooled crepes may be refrigerated for up to 48 hours, or frozen for several weeks prior to use. Separate cooled crepes with waxed paper inside a large zipper bag, carefully squeezing air out of bag before closing. Lay package flat to freeze. Completely thaw frozen crepes before use.*

LEMON DREAM CREPES

Using a medium saucepan over low heat, melt butter. Stir in lemon peel, lemon juice, salt and 1½ cups sugar. Add beaten egg mixture, whisking continuously until mixture is shiny and thick. Remove from heat to cool completely.

Whip cream to stiff peaks with ¼ cup granulated sugar. Gently fold half of whipped cream into cooled lemon mixture.

Assembly:
Place crepes on serving platter and fill generously with lemon cream mixture. Fold over sides and top with remaining whipped cream. Add a lemon twist to garnish.

Yield: 18 to 20 servings

Sister says: These heavenly crepes are better than lemon meringue pie, and easier!

½ cup butter

1 teaspoon lemon peel, grated

½ cup fresh lemon juice

Dash salt

1½ cups sugar

3 whole eggs and 3 egg yolks, lightly beaten

1 cup heavy cream

¼ cup sugar

18–20 prepared crepes (page 40)

Thinly sliced lemon for garnish

CHICKEN DIVAN CREPES

¼ cup butter

¼ cup flour

2 cups chicken broth

2 teaspoons Worcestershire sauce

3 cups extra-sharp cheddar cheese, grated

2 cups sour cream

2 (10-ounce) packages frozen broccoli spears, cooked and well drained

or

1½ pounds fresh broccoli, cooked and well drained

3 cups chicken, cooked and shredded

12 prepared crepes (page 40)

Melt butter in saucepan over medium heat and add flour, whisking briskly until mixture is bubbly. Add chicken broth and Worcestershire sauce, stirring constantly until thickened. Add half of the grated cheddar, stirring until cheese melts and sauce is well combined. Set aside to cool, approximately 30 minutes. Place sour cream into a medium bowl and add warm cheese sauce, stirring well.

Preheat oven to 350°F.

Butter two 9 x 13-inch casserole dishes.

Assembly:
Divide prepared broccoli and chicken in half. Place 2 broccoli spears (end to end) on each crepe, followed by 2 generous tablespoons of shredded chicken, evenly distributed. Spoon 2 tablespoons of cheese sauce over chicken and broccoli. Fold one side over filling followed by the other. Add a teaspoon of cheese sauce to secure the top fold.

Continue in this manner until there are 6 filled crepes in each pan. Pour any remaining cheese sauce down the center of the filled crepes and sprinkle with remaining grated cheddar. Cover pans loosely with aluminum foil. Bake until crepes are hot, approximately 20 to 30 minutes.

Yield: 6 servings

Sister says: Don't be intimidated by crepes. They are versatile, easy to make ahead and always a crowd-pleaser. Enjoy!

CHICKEN DIVAN CREPES

SMOKED SALMON CREPES

1 (8-ounce) package cream cheese, softened

4 tablespoons sour cream

¼ teaspoon salt

¼ teaspoon black pepper

2 tablespoons chives, minced

1½ tablespoons prepared horseradish

12 prepared crepes (page 40)

12 very thin slices premium smoked salmon

Paprika

Parsley

Using a small mixing bowl, stir cream cheese, sour cream, salt, pepper, chives and horseradish until smooth and well combined.

Assembly:
Spread cream cheese mixture evenly on each crepe. Add a thin slice of salmon and roll from one edge to the other (like a jelly roll). Place salmon crepes in tightly covered container and refrigerate for 3 to 4 hours or overnight.

Slice each cold salmon crepe into 4 or 5 crosswise pieces and arrange on serving platter. Sprinkle with paprika and garnish with parsley.

Yield: 48 appetizers

Sister says:

Presentation is a key element of any menu. Parsley sprigs are always pretty, but chopped parsley strewn like edible confetti is one of my favorite ways to garnish. Zigzag cut lemons or thin lemon twists are great with seafood, and mint sprigs and edible flowers are great for desserts. Charlotte and I love sugared rose petals for chocolate cake!

STRAWBERRIES & CREAM CREPES

3 cups fresh ripe strawberries, washed & stemmed

¾ cup sugar

1 cup heavy cream

1 cup sour cream

1 cup powdered sugar

12 prepared crepes (page 40)

Choose 12 perfect berries for garnish and set aside. Slice the remaining strawberries (bite-size pieces) into a large bowl; toss with sugar.

Using small bowl of mixer, beat cream at high speed into soft peaks. Do not overbeat. Add powdered sugar and then sour cream, beating on medium until well combined.

Make strawberry fans: Using a sharp paring knife, grasp the stem of each reserved strawberry and make 4 slices toward the stem, being careful not to cut all the way through the top. Gently spread the slices to form a fan.

Assembly:
Divide sliced strawberries among crepes and top with cream mixture. Fold over each side, and arrange filled crepes on serving platter. Place a dollop of cream mixture atop each crepe and garnish with a strawberry fan.

Yield: 12 servings

MELON MÉLANGE

Cantaloupe melon

Honeydew melon

2 kiwifruits

1 cup seedless grapes, washed

Mint

⅓ cup melon liqueur

1 tablespoon sugar

Halve each melon, remove seeds and carefully scoop bite-size balls into a large serving bowl with grapes. (Taste melon for sweetness.) Peel kiwifruit, slice into ¼-inch rounds and add to melon balls.

Using a small mixing bowl, crush several mint leaves. Sprinkle with sugar (add more if melons are not very sweet) and add melon liqueur. Stir to dissolve sugar. Pour over fruit and toss gently.

Cover tightly and refrigerate until ready to serve. Garnish with mint sprigs.

Yield: 4 to 6 servings

Sister says: Sweet and refreshing, this fruit compote is a perfect way to start your day.

SISTER'S BEEF TENDERLOIN ROLLS

24 Sister Schubert's Parker House Rolls, thawed

1 cup sour cream

⅓ cup prepared horseradish

¼ teaspoon salt

1 tablespoon lemon juice

1 tablespoon fresh basil, chopped

24 slices prepared beef tenderloin

Preheat oven to 375°F.

Using a medium mixing bowl, combine sour cream, horseradish, salt, lemon juice and basil.

Remove rolls from pan. Open each roll gently and place 1 teaspoon of mixture inside. Place one slice of tenderloin on mixture. Close rolls and return to pan.

Cover pan with aluminum foil and bake for 15 to 20 minutes.

Yield: 24 servings

TOMATOES PROVENÇAL

- 2 large ripe tomatoes
- Salt and pepper
- ½ cup fresh bread crumbs*
- ¼ cup Parmesan cheese, grated
- 1 clove garlic, pureed
- ¼ cup fresh basil, chopped
- 2 tablespoons black olives, chopped
- 2 tablespoons scallions, finely chopped
- 3 tablespoons olive oil

Preheat oven to 350°F.

Butter a medium baking dish.

Halve tomatoes and remove seeds and membranes. Rub cavities with sea salt and invert on paper towels to drain.

Using a medium mixing bowl, gently combine bread crumbs, cheese, garlic, basil, olives and scallions. Sprinkle lightly with olive oil, tossing and adding oil until mixture is well combined.

Lightly dry tomatoes with paper towels. Stuff tomatoes with crumb mixture. Drizzle sparingly with olive oil and bake until crumbs are lightly browned and tomatoes are hot, approximately 20 to 25 minutes.

Yield: 4 servings

Sister says:

Make your own delicious bread crumbs with leftover rolls. Simply slice rolls thin and bake in a 250-degree oven for 15 minutes, turning bread halfway through the baking time. Crumble by hand for coarse crumbs or process briefly in your food processor for finer crumbs. Stale bread makes stale crumbs, so use fresh leftovers only!

AUNT CHARLOTTE'S QUICHE LORRAINE

2 (9-inch) pastry shells, partially baked

1½ tablespoons butter

½ cup onion, finely chopped

5 eggs plus 1 yolk

2½ cups heavy cream

¼ teaspoon grated nutmeg

½ teaspoon salt

Dash cayenne pepper

1 package bacon, cooked, drained and crumbled

1 cup extra-sharp cheddar cheese, grated

1 cup Monterey Jack cheese, grated

Sister says:

This rich, flavorful quiche can be served for lunch or in smaller portions, as appetizers. The tender egg custard does not freeze well, but leftovers are rarely a problem!

Sauté onion in butter until transparent; set aside.

Using a large mixing bowl, whisk eggs until light, then add cream, nutmeg, salt and cayenne pepper, whisking until well combined.

Divide sautéed onion, bacon and cheeses between the 2 pastry shells. Carefully pour custard mixture into shells. (Do not overfill.)

Bake on center rack of oven until quiches are light brown and puffy, approximately 35 to 40 minutes. Slice quiche into wedges and serve hot.

Yield: Each quiche serves 6

CHEESY SHRIMP AND GRITS

Using a large pot, combine grits, cream, chicken stock, salt and water, and bring to a boil. Cook until creamy, according to package directions and set aside.

Sauté bacon until crisp; drain on paper towels, then crumble. Using skillet with reserved bacon grease, sauté tomatoes over medium heat until softened. Add garlic, chopped green onion and shrimp. Sauté until shrimp turns pink (approximately 3 to 4 minutes), sprinkle with juice of half a lemon and remove from heat.

Return grits to low heat and add butter, cheeses and crumbled bacon, stirring until cheeses melt. Spoon grits into rimmed soup bowls, top with hot shrimp mixture and garnish with chopped parsley and lemon slices.

Yield: 4 servings

Sister says: A word about tasting: Do it! I always taste for seasoning correction, sweetness and overall flavor. Get into the habit of tasting as you go, *and make these recipes your own.*

1½ cups quick-cooking grits

1 cup heavy cream

4½ cups chicken stock

2 cups water

1 teaspoon salt

1 pound fresh shrimp (peeled, deveined, and tails removed)

½ cup butter

1 (8-ounce) package cream cheese

1½ cups extra-sharp cheddar cheese, grated

8 slices bacon

2 to 3 cloves garlic, minced

2 dozen cherry tomatoes, whole

2 lemons (1 halved, the other sliced into thin rounds)

5 or 6 green onion tops, coarsely chopped

1 bunch flat-leaf parsley, coarsely chopped

Salt and pepper to taste

GAZPACHO SHOTS WITH MINI CORNBREAD MUFFINS

- 1 pound ripe tomatoes, peeled and quartered
- 2 cups premium tomato juice
- ½ cup bell pepper, seeded and coarsely chopped
- 1 cup cucumber, peeled and chopped
- 1 tablespoon olive oil
- 2 tablespoons cider vinegar
- 2 tablespoons onion, grated
- 1 tablespoon Worcestershire sauce
- 2 cloves garlic, minced
- Juice of 2 lemons
- Green hot pepper sauce to taste
- Salt and pepper to taste
- Cilantro
- Small carton sour cream

Combine all ingredients except cilantro and sour cream in bowl of food processor. Process very briefly for a medium chop consistency. Process again for finely chopped vegetables. Taste to correct for seasoning and consistency. Refrigerate for at least 4 hours or overnight.

To serve: Assemble at least a dozen shot glasses. Stir gazpacho and fill glasses three-quarters full. Top with a small dollop of sour cream and a sprig of cilantro.

Yield: 4 to 8 servings

See page 76 for Sister's Southern Cornbread recipe.

Sister says: *Everyone loves this zesty, refreshing cold soup accompanied by warm, sweet corn mini-muffins. You'll need lots of shot glasses!*

GRAPEFRUIT & AVOCADO SALAD WITH POPPY SEED DRESSING

Spring mixed greens, washed and dried on paper towels

3 Ruby Red grapefruit, peeled and sectioned

¾ cup sugar

1 teaspoon dry mustard

⅓ cup cider vinegar

1 teaspoon sea salt

1 cup canola oil

1 teaspoon poppy seeds

2 ripe avocados, peeled, pitted and sliced into wedges*

Place a small mound of salad greens on each plate. Arrange grapefruit sections in the center of the greens.

Using a medium mixing bowl, combine sugar, mustard, vinegar, salt, and oil, beating with a whisk until ingredients are well combined. Gently stir in poppy seeds.

*To prevent avocado slices from turning brown, wait until just before serving to peel and slice. Arrange avocado slices around outside of grapefruit and drizzle liberally with poppy seed dressing.

Yield: 4 to 6 servings

SAUSAGE ROLL BREAKFAST CASSEROLE

1 pan Sister Schubert's Sausage Rolls, thawed

8 large eggs

1 teaspoon dry mustard

2 teaspoons salt

1 teaspoon black pepper

2 teaspoons Worcestershire sauce

4 cups half-and-half

1 teaspoon hot pepper sauce

2 cups extra-sharp cheddar cheese, grated

2 tablespoons butter

Sister says:

This easy, delicious breakfast casserole is assembled the night before and baked in the morning for a fast and fabulous start to any day of the week. You may add sautéed onions and peppers to the custard for a tangy variation. My family loves this breakfast casserole, and I think yours will too!

Butter a 9 x 13-inch casserole dish.

Remove rolls from pan and slice each roll into thirds, cutting across sausage. Set aside.

Using a large mixing bowl, whisk eggs until light and frothy. Add mustard, salt, pepper, Worcestershire sauce, hot pepper sauce and half-and-half, whisking until ingredients are well combined. Place sliced rolls into prepared casserole. Sprinkle with grated cheese and pour egg mixture over cheese. Dot surface with butter, then cover tightly and chill for 8 hours or overnight.

Preheat oven to 350°F.

Bake until center is set, approximately 55 to 60 minutes. Let stand 5 minutes before serving.

Yield: 6 servings

SISTER'S STICKY BUNS

Combine 1 cup water, ¼ cup sugar, and ½ cup butter in a saucepan; heat until butter melts, stirring occasionally. Cool to 105°F to 115°F.

Combine yeast, warm water, and 1 teaspoon sugar in a 1-cup liquid measuring cup; let stand 5 minutes. Combine butter mixture and yeast mixture. Add egg; stir well.

Combine yeast mixture, 2 cups flour, and salt in a large bowl. Add remaining 2½ cups flour, ½ cup at a time, stirring vigorously until dough is no longer sticky and pulls away from the sides of bowl. Brush or lightly rub dough with some of the melted butter. Cover loosely, and let rise in a warm place (85°F), free from drafts, for 1 hour or until doubled in bulk.

Combine ½ cup melted butter, 1 cup brown sugar, corn syrup, and pecans; sprinkle mixture evenly in bottom of a well-greased 13 x 9 x 2-inch pan. Set pan aside. Combine remaining ½ cup brown sugar, remaining ¼ cup sugar, and cinnamon in a small bowl; set aside.

Punch dough down; turn out onto a well-floured surface. Roll dough into an 18 x 15-inch rectangle. Brush dough generously with some of the remaining melted butter; sprinkle evenly with cinnamon mixture. Roll up dough jelly-roll fashion, starting at the long side. Cut roll into 12 (1½-inch) slices. Place slices, cut sides down, in prepared pan. Brush slices with remaining melted butter. Cover loosely with a damp tea towel, and let rise in a warm place, free from drafts, for 1 hour or until tops of rolls rise just above top of pan.

Preheat oven to 350°F.

Bake rolls, uncovered, for 18 to 22 minutes or until golden. Cool in pan on a wire rack for 8 minutes. Invert pan onto wax paper; let rolls stand, covered with pan, for 1 minute. Remove pan, scraping any remaining pecan mixture from pan onto rolls. Serve warm.

Yield: 1 dozen

1 cup water

½ cup sugar, divided

½ cup butter

1 package active dry yeast

½ cup warm water (105°F to 115°F)

1 teaspoon sugar

1 large egg, lightly beaten

4½ cups all-purpose flour, divided

1 teaspoon salt

1 cup butter, melted and divided

1½ cups firmly packed brown sugar, divided

½ cup light corn syrup

1½ cups pecans, coarsely chopped

1 tablespoon ground cinnamon

Sister says: These rolls are so gooey and delicious, they're worth every ounce of effort it takes to prepare them. As a pretty substitute for chopped pecans, I like to use small, whole pecans. Mama says that the small pecans are more flavorful to boot!

FLY-OFF-THE-PLATE PANCAKES

1 cup all-purpose flour

1 tablespoon baking powder

1 tablespoon sugar

¼ teaspoon salt

1 large egg, lightly beaten

1 cup milk

2½ tablespoons sour cream

2 tablespoons butter, melted

Vegetable oil

Combine flour, baking powder, sugar and salt in a large bowl, stirring well to distribute ingredients evenly.

Combine egg, milk, sour cream and butter, stirring with a wire whisk until frothy; add to dry ingredients, stirring just until smooth. Allow batter to rest for 10 minutes.

Heat a large griddle or skillet to medium-high (375°F). The cooking surface for pancakes should not be greasy. Apply a little oil between batches and lightly wipe off with a paper towel.

For each pancake, pour ¼ cup batter onto hot surface. Cook pancakes until tops are covered with bubbles and edges are set; turn and cook other side.

Serve warm with butter and syrup or honey, if desired.

Yield: About 1 dozen

Sister says: *These tender, light-as-a-feather pancakes were Gommey's favorite breakfast bread. The secret ingredient is time! Baking powder interacts with the liquids to form a light, frothy batter which will produce excellent pancakes for the patient cook who will wait for them to work together. Resist the urge to make large pancakes; these really do fly off the plate if you follow my recipe!*

FLY-OFF-THE-PLATE PANCAKES

STEEL-CUT IRISH OATMEAL WITH MAPLE BACON

1 canister Irish steel-cut oatmeal

Water

Salt

Butter

Prepare traditional Irish oatmeal per package directions, approximately 35 minutes before serving. Serve hot with a generous dollop of butter and a small pitcher of buttermilk or cream on the side. A rasher of Maple Bacon completes this nutritious and delicious cereal.

Maple Bacon

1½ pounds thick-sliced premium bacon
Maple syrup
Dark brown sugar

Preheat oven to 425°F.

Line a rimmed baking pan with parchment paper.

Separate bacon slices and place on prepared baking pan. Brush each slice with maple syrup, and sprinkle liberally with brown sugar. Bake 10 minutes. Remove pan from oven and drain fat. Return to oven for 7 to 8 minutes. Drain on wire rack.

Yield: 6 servings

Sister says:

This healthy old-fashioned oatmeal is simply the best, and requires only a dab of butter and a splash of buttermilk or cream. Fresh blueberries or strawberries, a spoonful of local honey or a sprinkling of cinnamon sugar are all wonderful accents for oatmeal. When you add a few pieces of this divine bacon, you will be transported to breakfast heaven. I dare you to eat just two slices!

GRAPE CHICKEN SALAD CANAPÉS

6 chicken breasts (baked with tarragon, lemon pepper, salt, Greek seasoning, Worcestershire sauce and lemon juice), coarsely chopped

1½ cups celery, finely chopped

⅓ cup sweet pickle relish

2 eggs, hard-boiled, finely chopped

½ cup premium mayonnaise

4 tablespoons chicken broth

1 cup green seedless grapes, halved

½ cup Gruyère cheese, softened

1 pan Sister Schubert's Parker House Rolls, split and toasted

1 cup sliced toasted almonds

Combine chicken, celery, pickle relish, hard-boiled eggs, mayonnaise, chicken broth and grapes, tossing gently until well combined. (Add more mayonnaise if you like a wetter salad.)

Spread Gruyère on toasted rolls; top with 1 heaping tablespoon chicken salad and a sprinkle of toasted almonds.

Yield: 32 canapés

ARTICHOKE & HAM BRUSCHETTA

6 Sister Schubert's Dinner Yeast Rolls

6 tablespoons extra-virgin olive oil

Salt and pepper

2 (6½-ounce) jars marinated artichoke hearts, drained

4 ounces ham (or prosciutto), chopped

½ cup red onion, finely chopped

2 scallions, finely chopped

3 tablespoons olive oil

1 teaspoon fresh basil, sliced in thin ribbons

½ cup Parmesan cheese, shaved

Balsamic vinaigrette

6 basil leaves for garnish

Sister says:

Prosciutto is preferred for this savory appetizer, but a good smoked ham works fine. Cutting the olive oil with canola oil in even proportions keeps the flavor, but is less apt to burn. Serve as appetizers or as open-faced sandwiches for lunch—either way, I know that you will enjoy them.

Preheat oven to 350°F.

Slice rolls in half and place on baking sheet. Brush each slice with olive oil and lightly season with salt and pepper. Bake until a toasted golden brown. Remove from oven and cool on wire rack.

Cut artichoke hearts lengthwise into ¼-inch slices. Using a medium skillet, sauté artichokes, prosciutto and onion in oil until artichokes are golden and onion is transparent, approximately 4 minutes. Add scallions and sliced basil, stirring until well combined.

Spoon hot artichoke mixture onto toasted rolls, drizzle with balsamic vinaigrette and top with shaved Parmesan cheese. Garnish each bruschetta with a fresh basil leaf.

Yield: 12 appetizers

ROASTED VEGETABLE SANDWICHES WITH HERB GARLIC ROLLS

Place peppers on hot grill and cook until tender and charred, turning halfway to char both sides. Cool roasted peppers, then peel and slice. Brush onion, eggplant, zucchini, and squash with olive oil and sprinkle with salt, pepper and thyme. Grill vegetables until tender and charred, approximately 3 minutes on each side. Sprinkle roasted vegetables with a bit more olive oil and serve on Herb Garlic Rolls.

Herb Garlic Rolls

4 cloves garlic, minced
½ cup each fresh parsley, basil and thyme, chopped together
½ cup unsalted butter, melted
½ cup extra-virgin olive oil
1 package Sister Schubert's Dinner Yeast Rolls

Preheat oven to 325°F.

Using a small mixing bowl, combine garlic, herbs, butter and olive oil, blending well. Slice frozen dinner rolls in half and brush butter mixture on each slice. Bake until golden brown and toasted, approximately 12 minutes. Prepare sandwiches with roasted vegetables.

Yield: 10 sandwiches

---

2 red bell peppers

2 large sweet onions, thickly sliced

2 zucchini, thickly sliced

2 yellow squash, thickly sliced

1 eggplant, thickly sliced

Olive oil

Salt and pepper

1 tablespoon dried thyme

EASY COFFEE CAKE

½ cup chopped pecans

¼ cup sugar

1 tablespoon ground cinnamon

1 tablespoon butter, softened

2 cups all-purpose flour

1 tablespoon baking powder

½ teaspoon salt

½ cup sugar

1 teaspoon ground cinnamon

½ cup butter

1 large egg, lightly beaten

1 cup milk

1 teaspoon vanilla extract

Preheat oven to 350°F.

Grease and flour a 9-inch square pan; set aside.

Combine first 4 ingredients in a small bowl, stirring with a fork until crumbly. Set aside.

Combine flour and next 4 ingredients in a large bowl stirring until well mixed; cut in ½ cup butter with pastry blender until mixture resembles coarse meal. Combine egg, milk, and vanilla; add egg mixture to flour mixture, stirring just until dry ingredients are moistened.

Pour batter into prepared pan; sprinkle evenly with pecan mixture. Bake coffee cake for 30 to 35 minutes or until a wooden pick inserted in the center comes out clean. Cool in pan on a wire rack for 10 minutes. Cut into squares and serve warm with butter.

Yield: One 9-inch coffee cake

Sister says: This yummy coffee cake is truly easy to prepare and one of Gommey's "quick bread" recipes. If you want to gild the lily, drizzle with simple icing of powdered sugar and milk.

GARLIC SHRIMP CROSTINI

- 1 (8-ounce) package cream cheese, softened
- 2 tablespoons sour cream
- 1½ teaspoons Worcestershire sauce
- Juice of 1 lemon
- 3 tablespoons green onion, finely chopped
- 2 cloves garlic, minced and divided
- ½ teaspoon cayenne pepper
- 24 large shrimp, washed, shelled and deveined
- 2 tablespoons butter
- 1 (12-ounce) jar red chili sauce
- 12 Sister Schubert's Dinner Yeast Rolls, split and toasted
- Parsley for garnish

Combine cream cheese, sour cream, Worcestershire sauce, lemon juice, green onions, 1 clove of garlic and cayenne, beating until well combined. Spread cream cheese mixture on toasted rolls.

Sauté shrimp in butter with remaining minced garlic until pink and firm, approximately 3 minutes. Add one shrimp to each roll; top with a dollop of red chili sauce. Garnish with a sprig of parsley or parsley confetti.

Yield: 24 crostini

PERFECT FRIED CHICKEN
Page 65

3

MAIN DISHES

"What's for dinner?" I don't know about you, but if you're anything like me, you have heard that phrase more than a few times and have not had an answer. With busy work schedules and after-school activities, who's at home preparing dinner as we all walk in the door at the end of the day? I like to think the dinner fairies might have the table set and the meal ready, but that never happens. That's why I try to plan ahead as far as possible, making simple preparations on the weekends when I have more time. I keep the basic ingredients—the ones I use most often—on hand, so I can whip up a good supper in less than an hour. The evening meal is the prime time for families to reconnect with each other, the time for children to talk about their achievements in school or to ask for help with problems. Sitting around the table, children learn the give-and-take of conversation, and they carry that valuable skill into the world with them.

Whether you're serving Chicken Velvet Soup (page 69), Shrimp Po'Boys (page 73), or a steaming bowl of George's Chili (page 66), the conversation and attention you provide will surely anchor a lasting sense of stability in your family. Encourage your children to prepare a meal or have them help you in the kitchen. Cooking together is a wonderful forum to chat freely about any topic that happens to float through the air. Stay connected, and who knows? You may be surprised at what you learn!

ROASTED STUFFED LEG OF LAMB WITH SHALLOT SAUCE

1 (6-pound) leg of lamb, boned and trimmed

½ cup olive oil

Stuffing:

1 cup bread crumbs from Sister Schubert's Parker House Rolls

½ cup fresh parsley, chopped

¼ cup fresh mint, chopped

6 scallions (white and green parts), finely chopped

½ cup butter, melted

1 large egg, lightly beaten

Sauce:

1⅓ cups dry white wine

2 cups beef broth

3 medium shallots, finely chopped

1 tablespoon fresh rosemary, chopped

½ cup butter, softened

Preheat oven to 450°F.

Oil a shallow roasting pan with olive oil. Sprinkle prepared lamb with salt and pepper.

Using a medium mixing bowl, combine bread crumbs, parsley, mint, scallions, butter and egg, mixing well. Spread stuffing in a thin layer over the surface of the lamb and roll as tightly as possible. Secure stuffed lamb with kitchen twine.

Place lamb rolled edge down in pan and insert meat thermometer at thickest part. Place roasting pan on center rack of oven and reduce temperature to 325°F. Roast lamb for approximately 2½ hours for rare to medium-rare, or 3 hours for well done. Cook until meat thermometer reads 145°F for medium-rare, 160°F for medium, or 170°F for well done. Allow the roast to rest for 15 to 20 minutes before carving.

Prepare sauce: Using a medium saucepan, sauté shallots in a little of the butter until transparent. Add wine, broth and rosemary, stirring over medium-high heat until volume is reduced by half. Just after lamb is removed from the oven to rest before carving, add remaining butter to sauce and swirl in the pan until butter melts. Stir gently and serve hot with sliced lamb.

Yield: 6 to 8 servings

PERFECT FRIED CHICKEN

Wash the chicken pieces in cool water and shake off excess water (do not dry or your flour mixture will not adhere). Sprinkle wet chicken with sea salt.

Combine flour, paprika and pepper in a heavy-duty zipper bag, shaking to mix ingredients. Add one or two pieces of chicken at a time and shake vigorously until thoroughly coated.

Heat shortening (1¼ inches deep) in a large (at least 12-inch) cast-iron skillet to 360°F–365°F or until a drop of water sizzles. Add meaty pieces first (thighs and legs) skin side down, then add remaining pieces, being careful not to overcrowd the pan. Fry chicken one side at a time, turning with tongs.

When chicken is light golden brown (15 to 20 minutes), reduce heat to medium and cover tightly. Cook until tender, approximately 25 minutes, removing the lid for the final 10 minutes. Drain fried chicken on paper towels and serve piping hot.

Yield: 4 servings

3- to 3½-pound broiler-fryer chicken, traditional cut

Sea salt

1 cup all-purpose flour

3 teaspoons paprika

3 teaspoons black pepper

2 to 2½ cups solid shortening

Sister says: You can't get more Southern than this fried chicken recipe! If you do not have a well-seasoned cast-iron frying pan, do not despair. Use any large heavy skillet with a lid, or even an electric skillet. Here are my secrets for perfect fried chicken: Use solid shortening, not cooking oil. Make sure the melted shortening is hot enough, and keep an eye on the temperature throughout cooking. Never use a fork to turn fried chicken; if you puncture the skin, the juices will run out and your chicken will be dry. You too can fry this delicious chicken…just try it!

GEORGE'S CHILI

2 pounds ground chuck

1¼ cups onion, finely chopped

4 cloves garlic, minced

1 teaspoon ground cumin

2 tablespoons canola oil

4 tablespoons chili powder seasoning

2–3 teaspoons sea salt

1 tablespoon sugar

1 (16-ounce) can tomato sauce

2 (28-ounce) cans diced tomatoes

2 tablespoons black pepper

Optional:
2 (15-ounce) cans red kidney beans

Using a large pot, combine beef, onion, garlic and cumin, cooking over medium heat until meat is browned and onions are tender. Drain excess fat.

Add spices, sugar and tomatoes, simmering over low heat for 45 minutes, stirring occasionally. Taste to correct seasoning. If you like, add well-drained kidney beans and simmer an additional 15 minutes. Do not overcook the beans.

Yield: 6 to 8 servings

Sister says: My husband, George, is a great cook, and this is his favorite chili recipe. When we have this rich chili, he serves it with my dinner rolls brushed with garlic butter and a slice of cheddar cheese in the center. Makes me long for October!

GEORGE'S CHILI

GRILLED PORK TENDERLOIN WITH SISTER'S BARBECUE SAUCE

½ cup peanut oil

⅓ cup soy sauce

¼ cup red wine vinegar

3 tablespoons lemon juice

2 tablespoons Worcestershire sauce

1 clove garlic, minced

1 tablespoon fresh parsley, finely chopped

1 tablespoon dry mustard

1½ teaspoons black pepper

Pork tenderloins, ¾ to 1 pound each

Combine all marinade ingredients, stirring to blend well.

Fold and tie the thin end of each tenderloin under to give meat an even thickness. Place tenderloins in large casserole. Pour all of marinade mixture over meat, cover tightly and refrigerate for 4 hours.

Drain tenderloins, and grill by indirect heat, turning once, for 20 to 30 minutes, or until meat thermometer inserted at thickest part registers 170°F. Allow meat to stand for 10 minutes before serving.

Yield: Each tenderloin serves 4

Sister's Barbecue Sauce

¼ cup olive oil
¼ cup canola oil
1 cup onion, finely chopped
5 cloves garlic, minced
4 cups premium ketchup
¼ cup Dijon mustard
5 tablespoons Worcestershire sauce
¼ cup red wine vinegar
¼ cup fresh lemon juice
¾ cup dark brown sugar
½ teaspoon black pepper
1 teaspoon salt
½ teaspoon paprika
1 teaspoon red pepper flakes

Using a large saucepan, sauté the onions and garlic in oil until tender and transparent.

Add remaining ingredients and cook over low heat, stirring occasionally, for 30 to 40 minutes. Cover tightly and refrigerate.

Yield: 1 quart

Sister says:

This recipe is great to make ahead for tailgating! Slice the grilled tenderloins, wrapping each tightly in aluminum foil. Bake my large dinner rolls, wrap them in foil and assemble the sandwiches at the game. Take your barbecue sauce in a quart jar, and don't forget lots of napkins!

CHICKEN VELVET SOUP

1½ quarts chicken stock

1 pint half-and-half

⅓ cup butter

¾ cup all-purpose flour

2 cups cooked chicken, diced

1 teaspoon sea salt

White pepper to taste

Parsley for garnish

Sister says:

Whenever someone in my family is ill, I get the call for Chicken Velvet Soup. This creamy nutritious soup is almost as good as a shot of penicillin, and much more enjoyable. If you like, add a handful of chopped pimiento or a sprinkle of grated cheddar, but do serve a warm Sister Schubert's Parker House Roll alongside!

Using a large pot, over low heat, stir chicken stock and half-and-half until warm, not hot.

Using a medium saucepan over medium-low heat, melt butter. Add flour, whisking constantly until slightly thick. Add half of the warm chicken stock and half-and-half mixture; whisk constantly until well blended. Pour the flour mixture into the chicken stock mixture, stirring until well combined.

Add diced chicken and season with salt and pepper to taste, stirring over low heat until thoroughly blended.

Ladle soup into bowls and garnish with a sprinkling of chopped parsley.

Yield: 9 cups

CHICKEN & SAUSAGE GUMBO

- 2 cups roux
- 2 pounds fresh okra, washed and thinly sliced
- 4 tablespoons canola oil
- 1 medium onion
- 2 stalks celery
- 1 medium bell pepper
- 2 cloves garlic
- 3 quarts warm water
- 1 (14.5-ounce) can tomatoes
- ½ teaspoon chili powder
- ½ teaspoon dried thyme
- ½ teaspoon dried basil
- 2 or 3 bay leaves
- 1 teaspoon seasoned salt
- 1 tablespoon Worcestershire sauce
- Salt, black pepper and cayenne pepper to taste
- 1 pound andouille sausage, cut into ¼-inch slices
- 2 pounds baked chicken, cut into bite-size pieces
- 1 cup chicken broth
- ½ cup fresh parsley, minced
- ½ cup green onion, finely chopped (bulb and leaves)
- Gumbo file (powdered sassafras leaves) for seasoning

How to make a roux:
The backbone of Creole cuisine, roux is simply a type of gravy made with flour and cooking oil. The method is straightforward, but if you accidentally burn your roux, throw it away and start over. For this recipe, heat 2 cups canola oil in a large heavy pot over medium heat. Add 2 cups all-purpose flour slowly to hot oil, whisking constantly. When thoroughly mixed, lower the heat and continue stirring until the roux is chocolate brown in color. Quickly pour finished roux into a quart jar or bowl to stop cooking. Important note: Always dissolve roux into warm liquid; cold water will cause it to curdle. Roux keeps well, with or without refrigeration.

Chop onion, celery, pepper and garlic. Using a large Dutch oven or pot, sauté okra in oil until tender, stirring constantly. Add chopped vegetables and just enough water to cover. Simmer 10 minutes. Add 2 cups of roux, 3 quarts of warm water, tomatoes, chili powder, thyme, basil, bay leaves, Worcestershire sauce, salt, black pepper and cayenne pepper. Bring to a low boil, making sure that roux has completely dissolved. Lower heat and simmer, stirring frequently, approximately 2 hours.

Add sausage, chicken and chicken broth to gumbo, stirring until well combined.

Serve gumbo with rice, topped with minced parsley and green onion. Garnish with a dash of gumbo file powder.

Sister says: *If Cajun cooking contains a secret ingredient, it has to be roux. Roux may be made with butter, margarine or cooking oil, but I prefer the latter because it does not burn as quickly. For seafood gumbo, add 2 pounds of fresh peeled shrimp and a cup of crabmeat (instead of chicken). Cook 30 minutes longer and skim excess fat. Laissez les bons temps rouler! (Let the good times roll!)*

CHICKEN & SAUSAGE GUMBO

EASY BARBECUED BRISKET

3- to 4-pound beef brisket

1 tablespoon celery salt

1 tablespoon onion salt

2 tablespoons garlic powder

6 ounces Liquid Smoke

6 ounces Worcestershire Sauce

1 recipe Sister's Barbecue Sauce

Black pepper to taste

Make a rub with celery salt, onion salt and garlic powder. Rub both sides of brisket. Place brisket in deep baking dish. Pour Liquid Smoke and Worcestershire Sauce over meat. Cover tightly and refrigerate overnight or for at least 4 hours.

Preheat oven to 275°F.

Cover brisket with foil, and bake for 5 hours. Remove from oven; skim fat and half of pan juices. Pour barbecue sauce over meat and return to oven. Bake uncovered 45 minutes. Remove brisket to serving platter and allow to rest for 20 minutes. Scrape pan and stir briskly. Reserve pan drippings for service. Carve brisket (against the grain) into thin slices and drizzle with reserved drippings.

Yield: 6 to 8 as a main course or 24 filled Sister Schubert's Dinner Rolls.

Sister says: This is one of my oldest and most treasured recipes, featuring all the flavor of grilled meat with the convenience of the oven. Prepare the meat the night before, start cooking after lunch, and your delicious dinner is ready and waiting when you are!

SHRIMP PO'BOYS WITH WHITE REMOULADE SAUCE

Preheat oven to 350°F.

Slice each baguette in half lengthwise and place on a rimmed baking sheet. Spread one side of each loaf with mayonnaise and place sliced provolone on the other. Bake until toasted and crispy, 10 to 12 minutes.

Pat greens dry with paper towels, and divide evenly between the toasted baguettes.

Using a large skillet, sauté shrimp in butter and Creole seasoning, turning once, until cooked through, approximately 3 to 5 minutes.

Top greens with warm shrimp and drizzle with White Remoulade Sauce. Slice each loaf into three parts and serve open faced or as po'boys.

Yield: 6 servings

White Remoulade Sauce

1 cup premium mayonnaise
⅓ cup Creole mustard
3 entire green onions, finely chopped
1 tablespoon fresh lemon juice
2 tablespoons tarragon wine vinegar
2 teaspoons fresh parsley, finely chopped
½ teaspoon paprika
3 cloves garlic, minced
½ teaspoon cayenne pepper
1 tablespoon fresh tarragon, finely chopped or ½ teaspoon dried tarragon
Salt to taste

Combine all ingredients and mix thoroughly. To store, place sauce in a glass container and refrigerate.

Yield: 1½ cups

---

2 pounds fresh large shrimp, peeled and deveined

1 tablespoon Creole seasoning or "essence"

3 tablespoons butter

2 French baguettes

Mayonnaise

4–6 slices provolone cheese

1½ cups baby spring greens, washed

1 batch White Remoulade Sauce

Sister says:

This recipe is a favorite with the men in my family, and is easy to adapt for tailgating. Cook the shrimp the day before and refrigerate, along with a jar of White Remoulade Sauce. Slice the French bread, spread with mayonnaise, wrap tightly and grab your bag of greens. Even without toasting, these sandwiches are amazing!

MAIN DISHES

COUNTRY BREAD
Page 93

4

BREADS

"Be gentle when you touch bread.
Let it not lie, uncared for, Unwanted.
So often bread is taken for granted.
There is such beauty in bread—
Beauty of sun and soil,
Beauty of patient toil.
Winds and rains caressed it,
Christ often blessed it.
Be gentle when you touch bread."

—Celtic Prayer

SISTER'S SOUTHERN CORNBREAD
Cornbread Batter

¾ cup butter, melted

1 cup sour cream

¾ cup buttermilk

2 tablespoons water

2 large eggs, lightly beaten

1½ cups self-rising white cornmeal

Sister says:

Perfect cornbread batter should be thin enough to pour and should not show the tracks of the spoon when you stir it. If the batter is too thick, just stir in a little additional buttermilk. If you want to make a pan of cornbread with this recipe, substitute a 9-inch pan greased with 1 tablespoon melted butter.

Preheat oven to 400°F.

Grease bottoms of mini-muffin pan with 1 tablespoon melted butter.

Combine remaining melted butter, sour cream, buttermilk, water and eggs, stirring to combine. Add cornmeal, stirring until moistened.

Pour batter into mini-muffin cups, filling three-quarters full. Bake until golden brown and puffy, approximately 12 to 15 minutes.

Yield: 8 servings

BROCCOLI CORNBREAD

Preheat oven to 350°F.

Lightly butter a 9 x 13-inch casserole.

Combine first 6 ingredients in a large bowl; add cornmeal and sugar, stirring until dry ingredients are moistened. Do not beat.

Pour batter into prepared baking dish. Bake for 40 to 45 minutes or until cornbread is golden brown and top is set.

Yield: 8 servings

*Substitute plain cornmeal for self-rising using the following formula: For each cup of self-rising cornmeal called for, substitute one cup plain cornmeal combined with 1½ teaspoons baking powder and ½ teaspoon salt.

4 large eggs, lightly beaten

1 (10-ounce) package frozen chopped broccoli, thawed

1 small onion, finely chopped

1 green onion, finely chopped

1 cup small-curd cottage cheese

½ cup butter, melted

1½ cups self-rising cornmeal*

1 teaspoon sugar

Sister says: This hearty cornmeal is perfect with barbecue or grilled meat. For a cheesy twist, add 1 cup grated sharp cheddar cheese to the batter before baking.

COUNTRY CORN MUFFINS

1¼ cups plain cornmeal

¾ cup all-purpose flour

1 tablespoon plus 1 teaspoon baking powder

¾ teaspoon salt

1 tablespoon sugar

2 large eggs, lightly beaten

1 cup milk

¼ cup vegetable oil

Preheat oven to 425°F.

Grease a cast-iron muffin pan.*

Combine first 5 ingredients in a large bowl. Combine eggs, milk, and oil; add to cornmeal mixture, stirring until dry ingredients are moistened.

If using a cast-iron muffin pan, place well-greased pan into the oven for 5 minutes or until grease sizzles. Spoon batter into hot pans, filling muffin cups two-thirds full.

*For regular muffin pans, spoon batter into greased pans, filling two-thirds full.

Bake for 12 to 15 minutes or until muffins are golden brown. Remove from pans immediately.

Yield: 1 dozen

Sister says: Gommey called this type of cornbread "egg bread" since the original corn cake was simply made of cornmeal and water, fried in a skillet. It would have been scandalous in many Southern kitchens to add flour to cornbread! Remember to fill any empty muffin cups half full of water before baking to distribute the heat evenly and prevent over-browning.

COUNTRY CORN MUFFINS

APPLESAUCE MUFFINS

1 cup butter, softened

2 cups sugar

2 large eggs

1 teaspoon vanilla extract

4 cups all-purpose flour

1 teaspoon ground cinnamon

½ teaspoon ground allspice

½ teaspoon ground cloves

¾ cup chopped pecans

1 (16-ounce) jar applesauce

2 teaspoons baking soda

Preheat oven to 400°F.

Beat butter at medium speed of electric mixer until creamy, approximately 5 minutes. Add sugar, beat well. Add eggs and vanilla; beat well. Set butter mixture aside.

Sift flour and next 3 ingredients together; stir in pecans.

Combine applesauce and baking soda, stirring until mixture is foamy; add to butter mixture alternately with flour mixture, beginning and ending with flour mixture. Beat at low speed just until blended after each addition.

Spoon batter into greased muffin pans, filling cups two-thirds full.

Bake for 12 to 15 minutes or until muffins are golden. Remove from pans immediately.

Yield: 2 dozen

Sister says: This is my favorite muffin trick: Use paper baking cups to line your muffin tins, but spray the insides of the paper cups with vegetable oil cooking spray. The muffins will come right out for a perfect presentation!

MUFFINS TROPICALE

- 2 cups all-purpose flour
- 2 teaspoons baking powder
- ¾ teaspoon baking soda
- ½ teaspoon salt
- ½ cup firmly packed light brown sugar
- 2 tablespoons sugar
- 1 large egg, lightly beaten
- 1 (8-ounce) can crushed sweetened pineapple, drained
- 1 cup sour cream
- ½ cup chopped macadamia nuts
- ⅓ cup vegetable oil

Preheat oven to 425°F.

Combine first 6 ingredients in a large bowl; make a well in center of mixture. Combine egg and remaining 4 ingredients; add to flour mixture, stirring just until dry ingredients are moistened.

Spoon batter into greased muffin pans, filling cups two-thirds full.

Bake for 20 to 24 minutes or until muffins are golden. Remove from pans immediately.

Yield: 1½ dozen

LEMON-BLUEBERRY MUFFINS

LEMON-BLUEBERRY MUFFINS

Preheat oven to 400°F.

Combine ¼ cup flour and brown sugar; cut in 2 tablespoons butter with a pastry blender until mixture resembles coarse crumbs. Set aside.

Toss berries with 2 tablespoons sugar, if desired; set aside. Combine lemon rind and 1 teaspoon sugar; set aside.

Beat softened butter at high speed of electric mixer until creamy, approximately 5 minutes. Add ½ cup plus 2 tablespoons sugar; beat well. Add eggs; beat well.

Combine remaining 2 cups flour, baking powder, and salt. Combine baking soda and buttermilk; add to butter mixture alternately with flour mixture, beginning and ending with flour mixture. Add lemon rind and beat at low speed just until blended. Gently fold in blueberries.

Spoon batter into greased muffin pans, filling cups three-quarters full. Sprinkle brown sugar mixture evenly over batter.

Bake for 15 to 18 minutes or until golden brown. Let stand 5 minutes in pans before serving.

Yield: 1 dozen

Sister says: I always taste berries to check for sweetness before adding extra sugar. To ensure that your blueberries remain whole and do not clump together in the batter, toss them in a zipper bag with flour, and fold into batter very gently.

2¼ cups all-purpose flour, divided

⅓ cup firmly packed brown sugar

2 tablespoons butter

1 cup fresh or frozen blueberries

2 tablespoons sugar (optional)

Coarsely grated rind of 2 medium lemons

1 teaspoon sugar

½ cup butter, softened

½ cup plus 2 tablespoons sugar

2 large eggs

½ teaspoon baking powder

½ teaspoon salt

½ teaspoon baking soda

1 cup buttermilk

BREADSTICKS WITH SISTER'S SPICY SEASONING SALT

1 teaspoon active dry yeast

½ cup warm water (105°F to 115°F)

1 cup all-purpose flour

¼ cup Parmesan cheese, grated

1 teaspoon Sister's Spicy Seasoning Salt

1 teaspoon minced garlic

½ teaspoon salt

½ teaspoon sugar

1 tablespoon olive oil

¼ cup Parmesan cheese, grated

Additional Sister's Spicy Seasoning Salt

Sister says:

Versatile and delicious, these crunchy breadsticks are great as appetizers or served hot with homemade soup. Enjoy!

Preheat oven to 350°F.

Line a large baking sheet with parchment paper. Set aside.

Combine yeast and warm water in a 1-cup liquid measuring cup; let stand for 5 minutes.

Combine flour and next 5 ingredients in a large bowl. Add yeast mixture, stirring until well blended. Turn dough out onto a well-floured surface; knead lightly 4 or 5 times.

Roll dough into a 14 x 8-inch rectangle; cut lengthwise into 8 equal strips using a sharp knife. Place strips on prepared baking sheet, and brush with olive oil. Sprinkle strips lightly with desired amount of Sister's Spicy Seasoning Salt and remaining Parmesan cheese.

Bake for 45 minutes or until breadsticks are lightly browned. Remove breadsticks from baking sheets, and allow to cool on wire racks.

Yield: 8 large breadsticks

Sister's Spicy Seasoning Salt

1 cup kosher salt
2 tablespoons dried parsley flakes
2½ teaspoons paprika
2 teaspoons dry mustard
1½ teaspoons garlic powder
1½ teaspoons onion powder
1½ teaspoons ground oregano
1½ teaspoons ground cayenne pepper
½ teaspoon ground thyme

Combine all ingredients. Store in an airtight container at room temperature.

Yield: 1¼ cups

BREADSTICKS WITH SISTER'S SPICY SEASONING SALT

ANGEL CORN STICKS

1 package active dry yeast

2 cups warm buttermilk (105°F to 115°F)

½ cup shortening, melted and cooled to 105°F to 115°F

1½ cups plain cornmeal

1 cup all-purpose flour

1½ teaspoons baking powder

1 teaspoon salt

½ teaspoon baking soda

1 tablespoon sugar

2 large eggs, lightly beaten

½ cup shortening, melted

Sister says:

The addition of yeast makes these corn sticks so light that you'll agree they're heavenly! If you do not have a corn stick pan, you may make muffins using a well-greased muffin tin.

Preheat oven to 450°F.

Grease corn stick pans.*

Combine first 3 ingredients in small bowl; let stand for 5 minutes.

Combine cornmeal and next 5 ingredients in a large bowl. Add yeast mixture and eggs, stirring until well blended. Let batter stand for 30 minutes. (Do not stir.)

*Grease corn stick pans by spreading 1 teaspoon melted shortening evenly over surface of each mold. Heat corn stick pans in a 450-degree oven for 5 minutes or until oil sizzles.

Spoon batter into preheated molds, filling each space half full.

Bake at 450°F for 12 to 15 minutes or until corn sticks are puffy and golden. Remove corn sticks from pans immediately. Serve warm.

Yield: 2 dozen

ANGEL BISCUITS

Combine yeast and warm water in a 2-cup liquid measuring cup; let stand for 5 minutes. Add warm buttermilk; stir well.

Combine flour and next 4 ingredients in a large bowl; cut in shortening with a pastry blender until mixture resembles coarse meal. Add yeast mixture, stirring with a fork just until dry ingredients are moistened.

Turn dough out onto a lightly floured surface, and knead 10 to 15 times or until dough is smooth and no longer sticky. Roll dough to ¾-inch thickness; cut with a floured 2-inch biscuit cutter. Place biscuits on an ungreased large baking sheet, and cover with a damp tea towel. Let rise in a warm place (85°F), free from drafts, for 30 to 45 minutes or until doubled in bulk.

Preheat oven to 400°F.

Bake biscuits, uncovered, for 15 minutes or until golden.

Yield: 1 dozen

- 1 package active dry yeast
- ¼ cup warm water (105°F to 115°F)
- ¾ cup warm buttermilk (105°F to 115°F)
- 2½ cups all-purpose flour
- ½ teaspoon baking powder
- ½ teaspoon baking soda
- ½ teaspoon salt
- 2 tablespoons sugar
- ½ cup shortening

Sister says: I have no less than five recipes for Angel Biscuits in my files, but my choice for the one to include in this book was easy—my great-aunt Charlotte's recipe. I will always remember her telling me, "The finest company ever to put their feet under my table is my family!"

MAMIE'S EVERYDAY BISCUITS

2 cups all-purpose flour

2 teaspoons baking powder

¾ teaspoon salt

¾ cup milk

¼ cup vegetable oil

½ cup all-purpose flour, divided

2 tablespoons vegetable oil

Preheat oven to 400°F.

Combine first 3 ingredients in a large bowl. Combine milk and ¼ cup oil; add to flour mixture, stirring with a fork just until dry ingredients are moistened.

Sprinkle ¼ cup flour evenly over work surface; turn dough out onto floured surface. Sprinkle dough with remaining ¼ cup flour. Roll or pat dough to ¼-inch thickness; fold dough in half. Roll or pat entire surface one time only to set the dough for cutting. (Dough should be slightly less than ½ inch thick.) Cut biscuits with a floured 1½-inch biscuit cutter.

Pour 2 tablespoons oil into one end of a 15 x 10 x 1-inch jelly roll pan, tilting pan slightly to keep oil pooled. Dredge each biscuit generously on both sides in pooled oil; arrange in pan, leaving about 1 inch of space between biscuits. Wipe out any leftover oil with a paper towel. Bake for 15 to 20 minutes or until golden.

Yield: About 1½ dozen

Sister says: When I was growing up, these biscuits were on our table every day. They are unusual in their small size and preparation with oil, but are very authentic Southern cuisine. I can still see Mamie cutting them out on a floury tea towel in Mama's kitchen just before dinner. I hope you like Daddy's favorite biscuits!

BUTTERMILK BISCUITS

2 cups all-purpose flour, sifted

2 teaspoons baking powder

½ teaspoon baking soda

½ teaspoon salt

½ cup butter

½ cup buttermilk

Sister says:

The best trick I can share with you about baking powder biscuits is this: Thoroughly mix the baking powder into the flour before adding any other ingredient. Baking powder is bitter, and if it is not well incorporated, your biscuit might bite you back!

Preheat oven to 375°F.

Combine first 4 ingredients in a large bowl; cut in butter with a pastry blender until mixture resembles coarse meal. Add buttermilk, stirring with a fork just until dry ingredients are moistened.

Turn dough out onto a lightly floured surface, and knead lightly 3 or 4 times. Roll or pat dough to ½-inch thickness; cut with a floured 2-inch biscuit cutter.

Place biscuits on a lightly greased large baking sheet. Bake for 12 to 15 minutes or until golden.

Yield: About 1½ dozen

CLASSIC FRENCH BREAD

1½ packages active dry yeast

2 cups warm water (105°F to 115°F)

1 tablespoon sugar

3 cups bread flour, divided

2 tablespoons butter, melted

1 tablespoon salt

3 cups all-purpose flour

2 tablespoons cornmeal

1 large egg white, lightly beaten

2 tablespoons water

Sister says:

Although French bread is a cornerstone of French cuisine, it is easy and rewarding to bake in your own kitchen. Longer rising times help develop the unique, subtle flavor of the bread. Never let yeast bread sit in the pan after baking or it will become soggy from steam accumulation at the bottom of the pan or baking sheet. Bon appétit!

Combine yeast, warm water and sugar in a small bowl; let stand for 5 minutes.

Combine yeast mixture, 2 cups bread flour, sugar, butter and salt in a large bowl, stirring vigorously until well blended. Add remaining cup bread flour and all-purpose flour, one cup at a time, stirring vigorously until dough pulls away from the sides of the bowl. Turn dough out onto a well-floured surface and knead until smooth and elastic (about 10 minutes). Place dough in a well-greased bowl, turning over to grease top. Cover loosely with a damp tea towel and allow dough to rise in a warm place (85°F), free from drafts, for 1½ hours or until tripled in bulk.

Punch down, cover loosely and allow to rise 30 minutes, or until almost doubled in bulk. Lightly grease a large baking sheet or bread pan; sprinkle with cornmeal and set aside.

Punch down and turn dough out onto a lightly floured surface. Knead gently 4 or 5 times and divide dough in half. Shape each portion of dough into a long, narrow loaf tapering at each end. Place loaves on prepared baking sheet, allowing 4 inches of room between loaves. Allow to rise in a warm place, free from drafts, for 30 minutes, or until doubled in bulk.

Preheat oven to 400°F.

Cut several slits (¼ inch deep) diagonally across top of each loaf using a razor blade or thin, sharp paring knife. Combine egg white and water and gently brush over loaves. Place baking sheet on middle rack of oven. Fill a shallow pan half full of boiling water (pour from teakettle) on bottom rack of oven. Bake until loaves are golden brown and sound hollow when tapped, approximately 35 to 45 minutes. Transfer loaves to wire racks to cool completely.

CLASSIC FRENCH BREAD

PECAN BREAD

- 3 cups all-purpose flour
- 1 tablespoon plus 1 teaspoon baking powder
- 1 teaspoon salt
- 1 large egg
- ¾ cup sugar
- 2 tablespoons vegetable oil
- 1½ cups milk
- 1 cup chopped pecans

Grease and flour a 9 x 5 x 3-inch loaf pan; set aside.

Combine first 3 ingredients in a small bowl. Set aside.

Combine egg, sugar, and oil in a large mixing bowl; beat at medium speed of an electric mixer until blended. Add flour mixture to sugar mixture alternately with milk, beginning and ending with flour mixture. Beat at low speed just until blended after each addition. Stir in pecans.

Pour batter into prepared pan; allow batter to rest for 20 minutes.

Preheat oven to 350°F.

Bake for 1 hour and 10 minutes or until a wooden pick inserted in center comes out clean. Cool in pan on a wire rack for 10 minutes; turn out onto wire rack, and allow to cool completely.

Yield: 1 loaf

COUNTRY BREAD

Combine yeast and 1 cup warm water in a small bowl; let stand for 5 minutes. Stir in remaining warm water, sugar, salt, and lemon juice.

Combine yeast mixture and 2 cups bread flour in a large bowl, stirring until well blended. Add remaining bread flour and 2½ cups all-purpose flour, ½ cup at a time, stirring vigorously until dough pulls away from sides of bowl.

Turn dough out onto a well-floured surface, and knead until smooth and elastic (6 to 8 minutes). Place in a well-greased bowl, turning to grease top. Cover loosely with a damp tea towel, and let rise in a warm place (85°F), free from drafts, for 45 minutes or until doubled in bulk.

Lightly grease a large baking sheet; sprinkle with cornmeal, and set aside.

Punch dough down; turn out onto a lightly floured surface, and knead lightly 4 or 5 times.

Divide dough in half. Shape each portion of dough into a round loaf, and rub each loaf with 1½ tablespoons additional flour. Place loaves on prepared baking sheet, allowing 4 inches of space between loaves. Cover loosely with a damp tea towel, and let rise in a warm place, free from drafts, for 45 minutes or until doubled in bulk.

Preheat oven to 400°F.

Using a very sharp blade, make 3 (⅛-inch-deep) horizontal cuts and 3 (⅛-inch-deep) vertical cuts in the top of each loaf to resemble a tic-tac-toe pattern. Bake for 25 to 30 minutes or until loaves are golden brown and sound hollow when tapped. Transfer loaves to wire racks, and allow to cool completely.

Yield: 2 loaves

2 packages active dry yeast

1¾ cups warm water (105°F to 115°F), divided

1 tablespoon sugar

2 teaspoons salt

1 teaspoon lemon juice or white vinegar

3 cups bread flour, divided

2½ cups all-purpose flour

2 tablespoons cornmeal

3 tablespoons additional all-purpose flour

Sister says:

These round rustic loaves have a crusty exterior and a tender interior like that of French bread. To ensure a good crust, you may place a glass baking dish half full of boiling water on the bottom rack of the oven.

LEMON-POPPY SEED BREAD

LEMON-POPPY SEED BREAD

Preheat oven to 350°F.

Grease bottoms only of two (8½ x 4½ x 3-inch) loaf pans. Set prepared pans aside.

Combine first 5 ingredients in a large bowl and blend well. Combine 2 cups sugar and next 5 ingredients in a mixing bowl; beat at medium speed of an electric mixer until well blended. Add liquid mixture to flour mixture, stirring just until dry ingredients are moistened.

Pour batter into prepared pans. Bake for 1 hour or until a wooden pick inserted in center comes out clean.

While bread is baking, combine powdered sugar, 2 teaspoons lemon rind, and lemon juice. Remove loaves from oven; drizzle immediately with lemon glaze. Cool in pans on wire racks for 10 minutes; turn out onto wire racks, and let cool completely.

Yield: 2 loaves

Sister says: Freshly grated lemon zest gives these sweet fragrant loaves their excellent flavor. Try to grate only the rind and not the white pith of the lemons.

3 cups all-purpose flour

2 teaspoons baking powder

¼ teaspoon salt

2 tablespoons poppy seeds

2 tablespoons coarsely grated lemon rind

2 cups sugar

1 cup vegetable oil

¾ cup milk

1 teaspoon vanilla extract

½ teaspoon almond extract

3 large eggs

2 cups powdered sugar, sifted

2 teaspoons coarsely grated lemon rind

¼ cup fresh lemon juice

GOMMEY'S BANANA BREAD

2 cups all-purpose flour

1 teaspoon baking soda

½ teaspoon salt

½ cup butter or shortening

1 cup sugar

2 large eggs

1½ cups overripe bananas, mashed

½ teaspoon vanilla extract

⅔ cup pecans, chopped

Preheat oven to 325°F.

Grease and flour two (8½ x 4½ x 3-inch) loaf pans.

Combine flour, baking soda and salt, stirring to distribute soda evenly. Beat shortening at medium speed of mixer until creamy; gradually add sugar, beating well. Add eggs, one at a time, beating just until yellow disappears after each addition. Add bananas and vanilla, beating until well blended. Gradually add flour mixture, beating until batter is wet throughout after each addition. Add pecans and stir gently to distribute evenly throughout batter.

Pour batter into prepared pans and bake until a cake tester inserted in the center of a loaf comes out clean, approximately 1 hour. Cool pans on wire racks for 10 minutes, then turn out on racks to cool completely.

Yield: 2 loaves

Sister says: Whenever I bake with raisins or nuts, I shake them in a bag with a little all-purpose flour before adding to the batter. This way, instead of clumping together, they remain separate in the bread. This is one of Gommey's favorite recipes and a wonderful way to use up bananas that are too ripe to eat out of hand. For best results, wait until your bananas turn completely soft and brown.

APPLESAUCE BREAD

Preheat oven to 350°F.

Grease a 9 x 5 x 3-inch loaf pan; line bottom of pan with wax paper. Set prepared pan aside.

Combine ¼ cup pecans, brown sugar, and ½ teaspoon cinnamon in a small bowl; set aside. Sift remaining ½ teaspoon cinnamon, flour, and next 5 ingredients together into a medium bowl.

Combine 1 cup sugar and remaining 4 ingredients in a large mixing bowl; beat at medium speed of an electric mixer until blended. Add flour mixture; beat 1 minute. Stir in remaining ½ cup pecans.

Pour batter into prepared pan; sprinkle with pecan mixture. Bake uncovered for 45 minutes, cover loosely with foil for remaining 15 minutes. Bread is done when a wooden pick inserted in center comes out clean.

Cool in pan on wire rack for 10 minutes; turn out onto wire rack, and allow to cool completely.

Yield: 1 loaf

¾ cup chopped pecans, divided

½ cup firmly packed brown sugar

1 teaspoon ground cinnamon, divided

2 cups all-purpose flour

1 teaspoon baking soda

½ teaspoon baking powder

½ teaspoon salt

½ teaspoon ground nutmeg

¼ teaspoon ground allspice

1 cup sugar

1½ cups applesauce

½ cup vegetable oil

3 tablespoons milk

2 large eggs

PEACH CRUNCH TEA BREAD

⅓ cup sugar

⅓ cup all-purpose flour

2 tablespoons butter, softened

1 tablespoon ground cinnamon

2 cups all-purpose flour

1 teaspoon baking powder

½ teaspoon baking soda

½ teaspoon salt

1 (8-ounce) package cream cheese, softened

½ cup butter, softened

1½ cups sugar

2 large eggs

½ cup milk

1 teaspoon vanilla extract

1 cup peach preserves

Preheat oven to 350°F.

Grease well and flour a 12-cup Bundt pan.

Combine first 4 ingredients, stirring with a fork until mixture is crumbly. Sprinkle sugar mixture evenly into bottom of prepared pan. Set aside.

Combine flour and next 3 ingredients in a small bowl stirring until well mixed; set aside.

Beat cream cheese and ½ cup butter at medium speed of an electric mixer until creamy, approximately 5 minutes; gradually add 1½ cups sugar, beating well. Add eggs, one at a time, beating just until yellow disappears after each addition. Add flour mixture to cream cheese mixture alternately with milk, beginning and ending with flour mixture. Beat at low speed just until blended after each addition. Stir in vanilla.

Pour half of batter into prepared pan. Spread peach preserves over batter, leaving a ½-inch border around side and middle of pan. (Preserves will stick to pan if spread to edges.) Pour remaining batter over preserves.

Bake for 1 hour or until a wooden pick inserted in center comes out clean. Cool in pan on a wire rack for 10 minutes; turn out onto wire rack to cool completely.

Yield: One 10-inch cake

Sister says: This delicious tea bread is baked in a Bundt pan instead of a loaf pan. The "crunch" is created by the baked-on streusel topping that crowns the bread when it is inverted. I like to place a small vase of fresh flowers in the center of the ring before serving.

PEACH CRUNCH TEA BREAD

CHERRY-CHEESE BREAD

2 (3-ounce) packages cream cheese, softened

1 large egg

2 cups self-rising flour

1 cup sugar

1 large egg, lightly beaten

¾ cup apple juice

¼ cup butter, melted

1½ cups pitted sour cherries, drained

½ cup pecans, chopped

Preheat oven to 350°F.

Grease and flour a 9 x 5 x 3-inch loaf pan; line bottom of pan with wax paper. Set aside.

Beat cream cheese at medium speed of an electric mixer until creamy. Add 1 egg; beat well. Set aside.

Combine flour with lightly beaten egg, apple juice and butter in a large bowl; stirring just until dry ingredients are moistened.

Pour half of batter into prepared pan; spread with cream cheese mixture. Top with remaining batter.

Bake for 1 hour and 10 minutes or until a wooden pick inserted in center comes out clean. Cool in pan on a wire rack for 10 minutes; turn out onto wire rack, and let cool completely.

Yield: 1 loaf

SISTER'S SCONES

Preheat oven to 375°F.

Combine first 4 ingredients in a large bowl. Cut in butter with a pastry blender until mixture is crumbly. Stir in raisins. Add 1 cup heavy cream, stirring with a fork just until dry ingredients are moistened.

Turn dough out onto a lightly floured surface, and knead lightly 10 to 12 times or until smooth and no longer sticky. Roll or pat dough to ½-inch thickness; cut with a floured 1-inch scalloped cookie cutter. Place scones on lightly greased large baking sheets, leaving 1 inch of space between scones. Brush scones with remaining 3 tablespoons whipping cream.

Bake for 15 to 20 minutes or until golden brown.

Yield: 40 scones

4½ cups all-purpose flour

2 teaspoons baking powder

½ teaspoon baking soda

3 tablespoons sugar

1 cup butter

1 cup golden raisins

1 cup plus 3 tablespoons heavy cream, divided

Sister says: For an extra-special flavor, soak raisins in brandy for one hour or until plump and rehydrated. Drain and shake with a little flour before adding to dough. This method keeps raisins separate in the bread and prevents clumping. I love to serve these pretty little scones at parties with lemon curd!

FOCACCIA

¾ cup warm water (110°F)

1 tablespoon sugar

1½ teaspoons active dry yeast

6 tablespoons olive oil, divided

2½ cups all-purpose flour

1 teaspoon sea salt

Olive oil

Sister says:

This venerable bread deserves an introduction: In ancient Rome, panis focacius *was a flat bread baked in the ashes of the fireplace in the center of the home. It was then, and is now, a savory bread with many uses. Focaccia is a great snack, a versatile appetizer and a good companion to many meals. Say "foe-cah-cha" and stand by for the compliments!*

Ideas for toppings: Coarse sea salt, fresh rosemary, freshly cracked black pepper, sun-dried tomatoes, thinly sliced red or yellow onion, sliced ripe olives, grated Parmesan or Romano cheese.

Combine water, sugar and yeast in a small bowl; set aside for 10 minutes. Stir in 2 tablespoons olive oil.

Combine 2 cups flour and 1 teaspoon sea salt in large bowl of mixer fitted with dough hook. Add yeast mixture and mix on medium-low speed for 5 minutes. Add remaining flour and continue mixing to form a very soft dough. Dough should hold together; if dough is too sticky, add a few tablespoons of flour and mix until consistency is correct.

Place dough in a well-oiled bowl; turn to coat top. Cover with a damp tea towel and allow to rise in a warm place (85°F), free from drafts, for 1½ hours or until doubled in bulk. Pour 2 tablespoons olive oil into a 10 x 15-inch rimmed baking pan. Transfer dough to the pan and gently stretch to cover the bottom of the pan. Dough may need to rest for a moment or two during this process. Try not to tear the dough.

Preheat oven to 425°F.

Cover dough loosely with a damp tea towel and allow to rise in a warm place for 15 to 20 minutes.

Remove towel and drizzle 2 tablespoons of olive oil over surface of dough. Using your fingertips, indent the surface of the focaccia and add your choice of toppings, gently pressing them into the indentations.

Bake for 20 to 25 minutes, or until focaccia is golden brown. Cool on wire rack. Brush with additional olive oil if desired.

Yield: One 10 x 15-inch focaccia

FOCACCIA

SOURDOUGH
Sourdough Starter

2 packages active dry yeast

1½ cups warm water (105°F to 115°F), divided

⅔ cup sugar

2 tablespoons instant potato flakes

Combine yeast and ½ cup warm water in a 1-cup liquid measuring cup; let stand for 5 minutes.

Combine yeast mixture, remaining 1 cup warm water, sugar, and potato flakes in a large bowl, stirring until well blended. Cover loosely with plastic wrap, and let stand in a warm place (85°F), free from drafts, for 8 hours. Starter is ready to use at this point. If not, refrigerate in a glass jar.

Feed starter every 3 days with:

1 cup warm water (105°F to 115°F)
⅔ cup sugar
3 tablespoons instant potato flakes

Stir gently, cover loosely and let stand in a warm place for 8 hours. Refrigerate after 8 hours.

Sister says:

Although it seems like a lot of trouble, working with sourdough starter is fun and easy to share. Give a jar of starter with a pan of freshly baked rolls and keep this old-fashioned recipe going!

Sister's Sourdough Dos and Don'ts

Do store sourdough starter in a glass or crockery container. Metal may adversely affect sourdough flavor.

Don't store sourdough starter in an airtight container. Remember: Starter is alive and growing, and it requires oxygen.

Do allow starter to come to room temperature and begin to bubble before using.

Don't rush the rising time for sourdough bread. It takes several hours for the natural fermentation of the potato water, sugar, flour and yeast to occur.

Do replenish, or feed, sourdough starter every three days per directions.

Do discard starter that has changed color or has developed mold.

MAMA'S SOURDOUGH BREAD

Combine first 3 ingredients in a large bowl.

Combine flour and salt in a large bowl. Add 2 cups flour mixture to starter mixture, stirring until well blended. Add remaining flour mixture to starter mixture, one cup at a time, stirring vigorously until dough holds together. (Dough will be very stiff.) Place dough in a well-greased bowl, turning to grease top. Cover loosely with a damp tea towel, and let rise in a warm place (85°F), free from drafts, for 6 hours or until doubled in bulk.

Generously grease two (9 x 5 x 3-inch) loaf pans; set aside.

Punch dough down; turn out onto a lightly floured surface, and knead until smooth and elastic (5 to 8 minutes). Divide dough in half. Roll each portion of dough into a 14 x 9-inch rectangle. Roll up dough, starting at short side, pressing firmly to eliminate air pockets; pinch ends to seal. Place dough, seam side down, into prepared pans.

Brush loaves with melted butter. Cover loosely with damp tea towels, and let rise in a warm place, free from drafts, for 6 hours or until dough rises above tops of pans.

Preheat oven to 350°F.

Bake loaves for 35 to 45 minutes or until golden and loaves sound hollow when tapped. Remove bread from pans immediately; cool completely on wire racks.

Yield: 2 loaves

1½ cups warm water (105°F to 115°F)

1 cup Sourdough Starter (page 104)

½ cup shortening, melted

6 cups all-purpose flour

1 teaspoon salt

3 tablespoons butter, melted

Sister says: Sourdough bread takes a long time to rise, but this is the secret to that great sour flavor. Here's my process: Remove the starter from the refrigerator in the morning and allow it to warm up and work all day. Before bed, make the dough and leave it to rise overnight. The next morning, prepare the loaves, leaving them to rise during the day. Then you're ready to bake delicious sourdough bread for dinner…it's easy and well worth the extra effort to prepare. Go ahead; try your hand at this wonderful old recipe!

SOURDOUGH ROLLS

1½ cups warm water (105°F to 115°F)

1 cup Sourdough Starter (page 104)

½ cup shortening, melted and cooled to 105°F to 115°F

6 cups all-purpose flour

1 teaspoon salt

½ cup butter, melted

Combine first 3 ingredients in a large bowl. Combine flour and salt in a large bowl. Stir 5 cups of flour mixture into starter mixture. Using your hands, incorporate remaining 1 cup flour mixture. Cover loosely, and let rise in a warm place (85°F), free from drafts, for 8 hours.

Grease four (8-inch) round cake pans; set aside.

Punch dough down; turn out onto a well-floured surface, and knead 10 times. Divide dough in half.

Roll 1 portion of dough to ½-inch thickness; cut into 32 rounds using a floured 2-inch biscuit cutter. Pull each round into an oval, approximately 2½ inches long. Dip 1 side of oval into melted butter. Fold oval in half with buttered side facing out.

For each pan, place the folds of 10 rolls against side of prepared pan, pressing center fronts of rolls together gently to seal. Place 5 rolls in inner circle, and 1 roll in center of pan for a total of 16 rolls per pan. Repeat entire procedure with remaining half of dough.

Cover loosely with a damp tea towel, and let rise in a warm place, free from drafts, for 6 hours or until doubled in bulk.

Preheat over to 375°F.

Bake rolls, uncovered, for 15 to 18 minutes or until lightly browned.

Yield: 64 rolls

Sister says:

Mama introduced me to baking with sourdough, and created the starter with directions shared from a dear friend. The long rising times create the distinctive sour flavor of this delicious bread. Mama taught me to make the dough before bed the night before baking, allowing the dough to rise overnight. Knead and cut them in the morning and the rolls will rise during the day in time to bake them for dinner.

SOURDOUGH ROLLS

COMMUNION BREAD
Page 113

5

THE BREAD OF LIFE

Baking bread has been a part of my life since I was a little girl. My grandmother, mother, and aunts were always sharing bread-making tips and secrets with each other, and I was listening when they spoke. I'm not sure what I found so fascinating about yeast and kneading tips, but I was drawn to their conversations and felt a kindred spirit in the kitchen.

For centuries, altar bread was prepared by dedicated members of the clergy who specialized in making the simple unleavened bread. Over the years, my thoughts on baking bread seem to have taken on a life of their own—I have come to believe that bread has a greater purpose than merely providing nourishment. It is a simple gift but such a pleasure to provide. My hands seem to be happiest when I am baking and especially so for the Communion Table. When I bake Communion Bread, I feel peaceful and reverent in the humble gift of bread. It could be the hands-on care it requires or the time involved in preparing it, but in my heart, it has become an almost spiritual experience, especially when I make what I call "Blessed Bread." The bread is not really blessed, but when I make it, I tend to focus on what it represents.

Some recipes call for only flour, salt, and water, while others allow additions like honey and baking soda. Check with your pastor and see if your church might enjoy homemade altar bread. Depending on the denomination, there are many possibilities, and your church may even have a preferred recipe.

There is no special ingredient that sets the bread apart, but rather, it is the history and the promise attached to the bread that allows me to focus on what is truly important—faith and family. In any case, I hope that you will try your hand at baking bread for your church.

CHALLAH

1 package active dry yeast

1 cup warm water (105°F to 115°F)

3 tablespoons sugar

1 tablespoon salt

3 tablespoons vegetable oil

5 cups all-purpose flour, divided

2 large eggs, lightly beaten

2 large egg yolks, lightly beaten

1 teaspoon water

1 tablespoon poppy (or sesame) seeds

Combine yeast and warm water in a 2-cup liquid measuring cup; let stand 5 minutes.

Combine sugar, salt, and oil in a large bowl; stir in 2 tablespoons flour. Stir in yeast mixture and 2 eggs. Add remaining flour, 1 cup at a time, stirring until dough pulls away from bowl.

Turn dough out onto a well-floured surface; knead until smooth and elastic (5 to 7 minutes). Place in a well-greased bowl, turning to grease top. Cover loosely with a damp tea towel; let rise in a warm place (85°F), free from drafts, for 1 hour or until doubled in bulk.

Punch dough down; turn out onto a lightly floured surface. Divide dough into thirds; roll each third into a 15-inch rope. Place ropes on a large greased baking sheet and braid, tucking ends under.

Combine egg yolks and 1 teaspoon water; brush over loaf. Sprinkle with poppy seeds. Cover loosely with a damp tea towel, and let rise in a warm place, free from drafts, for 45 minutes or until doubled in bulk.

Preheat oven to 375°F.

Bake for 30 to 35 minutes or until crust is golden and loaf sounds hollow when tapped. Remove loaf from baking sheet, and allow to cool on a wire rack.

Yield: 1 loaf

Sister says:

This traditional Jewish Sabbath bread is most commonly shaped into a short straight braid, but can be shaped into a braided wreath for Rosh Hashanah. For a sweet alternative, add 1 cup golden raisins to the dough just before shaping. Shalom!

CHALLAH

THE BISHOP'S BROWN IRISH SODA BREAD

13 ounces coarse whole wheat flour

1 ounce all-purpose flour

1 teaspoon salt

1 teaspoon baking soda

1 tablespoon dark brown sugar

1½ cups buttermilk

Sister says:

My friend, the Right Reverend Philip Duncan, Bishop of the Central Gulf Coast, was kind enough to share his favorite recipe for Brown Irish Soda Bread. The original Irish Soda Bread is made with white flour and no sweetener, but this chewy whole wheat version benefits from the addition of brown sugar. According to his wife, Kathy, traditional Irish bakers wrap their soda bread in a damp tea towel to keep moist until serving. Now you know!

Preheat oven to 400°F.

Grease a round cake pan well.

Combine dry ingredients, stirring until well mixed. Add buttermilk; mix by hand (do not knead).

Shape dough into a rough ball and scoop into prepared pan, flattening with the palm of your hand to a thickness of approximately 1½ inches. Using a knife dipped in flour, cut a cross into the top of the dough (to make it easy to break into quarters).

Bake at 400°F for 25 minutes; turn heat down to 350°F and bake 15 minutes longer. Turn out onto wire rack to cool. The bottom of the loaf will have a hollow sound when tapped to show that it is done.

Yield: 1 loaf

COMMUNION BREAD

Using a large bowl, mix flours together until evenly blended. Add warm water; stir briskly until dough begins to hold together and pulls away from the sides of the bowl. (There will be some unincorporated flour at this point.) Turn dough out onto lightly floured surface and knead until smooth and elastic, approximately 5 minutes. If dough remains sticky, add a little whole wheat flour. Cover dough with upside down bowl and allow to rest for 5 minutes.

Preheat oven to 450°F.

Divide the dough into 8 equal parts. Roll each piece into a ball, then press into a circle approximately 3¼ inches in diameter and ½ inch thick. Score each circle into 40 pieces (as shown in the photograph on page 108): cut the small circle first, using a 1-inch cutter (a donut-hole cutter works here), then the second circle, using a 2-inch biscuit cutter. Cut two straight lines at right angles across the circle (a cross), then cut each quarter of the two outer circles into thirds (2 cuts in each quarter). Cut each section in the outer circle in two. Try to cut almost through on each cut, so that the bread will break evenly.

Place loaves on parchment-lined baking sheets and bake until centers are firm and golden brown or approximately 15 to 18 minutes. Cool on wire racks.

Yield: 8 loaves or 320 pieces

4½ cups whole wheat flour

1⅓ cups all-purpose flour

2¼ cups warm water

Sister says: *This unleavened Communion Bread follows the traditional rule that the Host must be prepared with wheat flour and water only (no oil or sugar), which symbolizes Christ's sacrifice. Bake Communion Bread the day before it is used; wrap cooled loaves in plastic separated by wax paper. This beautiful handmade altar bread is far more interesting than little white wafers!*

UKRAINIAN COMMUNION WAFERS

4 cups bread flour, plus extra for dusting

1 teaspoon salt

1 cup warm water (110°F)

2 tablespoons butter, melted

In a large mixing bowl, combine flour and salt. Add water slowly, mixing to form a ball of dough. If the dough is sticky, add a few tablespoons of flour. Divide dough into 3 pieces and place on a lightly floured work surface. Cover with plastic wrap and allow the dough to rest for 30 minutes.

Preheat oven to 400°F.

Roll each ball of dough into a large thin oval and transfer to an ungreased baking sheet. Brush each wafer lightly with melted butter.

Bake for 10 to 12 minutes, or until wafers are crisp and golden. Allow wafers to cool on racks and break into desired pieces for Communion.

Yield: Varies

Sister says: *This extra-special recipe comes from Sasha's Home in Gorlovka, Ukraine, where my dear friend Irina "Ira" Grabko administers the Barnes Family Foundation program, which protects and provides care for a group of young orphans. Ira is my assistant, and along with many other duties, she provides Christian education and guidance for the children. When I asked Ira where she gets the Communion Wafers for Sasha's Home, she confided that she makes them herself, and shared this simple recipe. It reminds me that even in difficult times, where there's a will, there's a way.*

UKRAINIAN COMMUNION WAFERS

6

SIDES & VEGGIES

Vegetables! Every once in a while when I was a girl, Mama made a whole supper of baby butter beans, field peas, sweet corn, and tomatoes so tart and juicy we did not add a thing but our forks. She served them with hot, buttery cornbread and biscuits with homemade crab apple jelly. I loved those times! We would have laughed if anyone had used the word "vegetarian"—it was just summer supper to us.

I have gathered some of my favorite side dishes under the heading "Sides & Veggies," and I encourage you to experiment with them. Mix and match to create a menu that has personal flair, expressing your own good taste. Vegetables are no longer something you have to try to sneak into your child's diet. With creative ways to serve them, you will not have to say, "Eat your vegetables"; the kids will be asking for seconds. Why not try a night of vegetarian fare featuring Sister's Tomato Pie (page 123), Parmesan-Roasted Asparagus (page 119), a small salad, and of course, Sister Schubert's Homemade Rolls warm from your oven! Get creative; your family will love the change.

FRESH CORN FRITTERS

6 ears sweet corn, shucked

4 large eggs, lightly beaten

½ cup plus all-purpose flour

1 teaspoon salt

White pepper to taste

2 cups solid shortening

Carefully remove silk from corn. Cut corn over a large bowl to catch juices. Method: Using a sharp paring knife, slice down each vertical row of corn, cutting through to the cob. Cut corn away from cob; scrape liquid from cobs before discarding.

Add eggs, flour and seasonings to corn, stirring until well combined. Batter should be slightly thick, similar to pancake batter in consistency. If batter is too thin, add flour, a tablespoon at a time, stirring well after each addition.

Using a cast-iron skillet, melt shortening over medium-high heat until temperature reaches 325°F, or a droplet of water pops. (There should be enough oil to cover the fritters.)

Use a ⅓-cup measuring cup of batter per fritter and fry 4 fritters at a time. Fry until golden brown, turning halfway through, approximately 5 minutes each side.

Drain on paper towels and serve warm.

Yield: 10 fritters

Sister says: Fresh corn is hard to beat and this old-fashioned recipe really is a crowd pleaser. If you do not have a cast-iron skillet, an electric skillet works just fine.

PARMESAN-ROASTED ASPARAGUS

- 20 fresh asparagus spears
- ½ cup olive oil
- ½ cup canola oil
- 1½ cups Parmesan cheese, grated
- Sea salt
- Freshly ground black pepper

Sister says:

Thin asparagus and thick asparagus are simply different types, with no difference in tenderness. Both kinds are wonderful, don't you agree? These crisp, cheesy asparagus spears are great as appetizers too.

Preheat oven to 400°F.

Line a rimmed baking sheet with parchment paper.

Wash and remove woody stem ends from asparagus. Pat dry and place on prepared baking pan.

Combine oils and brush lightly over asparagus spears, turning to cover. Sprinkle with sea salt and freshly ground pepper, then with half of the Parmesan cheese. Cook for 20 minutes, turn, sprinkle with remaining cheese and return to oven for 15 minutes.

Yield: 4 servings

SISTER'S ARTICHOKE CRAB DIP

2 (15-ounce) cans premium artichoke hearts, well drained

1 cup Parmesan cheese, freshly grated

1 cup premium mayonnaise

1 pound lump crabmeat, carefully picked over

Preheat oven to 350°F.

Butter a medium casserole.

Rinse crabmeat in cold running water and drain in a colander. Puree ingredients in food processor. Pour crab mixture into prepared casserole and bake until golden brown and bubbly, approximately 30 to 35 minutes. Serve hot accompanied by Melba toast rounds.

Sister says: My family truly loves this appetizing combination of crabmeat, cheese and artichokes. No matter what they tell me at the seafood counter, I always carefully pick through the crabmeat to remove tiny bits of shell. If you have ever chewed a bit of crab shell, you know that this detail is critical to the success of your dish.

MAMIE'S POTATO SALAD

6–8 Yukon Gold (or Idaho) potatoes, peeled

1 small red onion, finely chopped

5 stalks celery, washed

3 eggs, hard-boiled, cooled and diced

½ cup sweet or dill pickle relish

1 cup premium mayonnaise

1 teaspoon prepared (yellow) mustard

1 or 2 teaspoons salt, to taste

1½ teaspoons white pepper

Using a large pot, simmer whole potatoes until cooked through, approximately 20 to 30 minutes. The potatoes should be tender and not mealy; slightly firm but done. Set aside to cool.

Remove strings from celery stalks and chop fine. (You should have at least 1 cup of chopped celery.) Using a medium bowl, combine celery, onion, relish, eggs, mayonnaise and mustard, stirring gently until well mixed. Season with salt and pepper to taste.

Dice cooled potatoes into ½-inch cubes and transfer to a large serving bowl. Gently dress the potatoes with the mayonnaise mixture, tossing to coat evenly. Cover tightly and refrigerate for at least 1 hour.

Yield: 6 to 8 servings

Sister says: There are as many ways to make potato salad as there are cooks, so feel free to add your favorite twist to this great old-fashioned recipe. Mamie would never have considered herself a gourmet cook, but she was a master of Southern cuisine who never referred to a written recipe. With a touch, she knew when meat was done, and with only her hands as measuring cups, she made perfect biscuits and pie crusts. When I was a child, Mamie would push the kitchen stool up to the stove so that I could "help" her fix dinner, and that is how I began my culinary career!

SISTER'S TOMATO PIE

- 1 (9-inch) pie crust
- 3 large (or 4 medium) ripe tomatoes, peeled and sliced ¼ inch thick
- 3 scallions, washed, chopped (including green tops)
- 1 cup premium mayonnaise
- 2 cups extra-sharp cheddar, grated
- ½ teaspoon pepper
- ½ teaspoon salt
- 1 sprig fresh basil, chopped

Preheat oven to 350°F.

Place pie crust carefully into deep-dish pie pan and flute or crimp the edges. Arrange sliced tomatoes inside crust followed by chopped green onions. Combine mayonnaise, grated cheese, basil, salt and pepper and spread over tomatoes and onions.

Bake until golden brown and bubbly, approximately 45 to 50 minutes.

Yield: 6 servings

Sister says:

There's something special about sun-ripened tomatoes! And they seem to ripen all at once in my garden. This rich, cheesy pie is a great side dish for summer supper, and a good way to enjoy those extra homegrown tomatoes.

SISTER'S FANCY COLESLAW

½ head green cabbage, julienned

¼ head red cabbage, julienned

½ green bell pepper, julienned

½ red bell pepper, julienned

½ yellow bell pepper, julienned

½ cup julienned carrot

1 green onion, top only, 1-inch dice

1 tablespoon fresh oregano, chopped or 1 teaspoon dried oregano

Salt and pepper to taste

¾ cup Marzetti's Slaw Dressing

Using a large bowl, combine vegetables with slaw dressing, tossing to coat well. Serve cold.

Yield: 8 to 10 servings

MAMA'S CHEESE STRAWS

Sift dry ingredients together and stir to blend well. Using large bowl of mixer on medium speed, blend cheese and butter until well combined. Add flour mixture a little at a time, kneading in the last flour addition. Work the dough by hand until soft and thoroughly blended.

Preheat oven to 350°F.

Line a baking sheet with parchment paper. Fill cookie press with dough and insert horizontal ridged template. Press an even line of dough, breaking 1 inch before bottom of pan. Using a sharp knife, cut dough at 2-inch intervals. Dust lightly with paprika. Bake until straws are golden, approximately 12 to 15 minutes. Do not brown! Cool on wire racks. When straws are completely cooled, transfer to wax-paper lined tin, separating layers with wax paper.

Yield: 3 dozen

16 ounces extra-sharp cheddar cheese, grated

½ cup butter, softened

2 cups all-purpose flour

1 teaspoon baking powder

1 teaspoon salt

½ teaspoon cayenne pepper

Paprika

Sister says: These tangy little treasures are always welcome at parties and they make an excellent gift as well. If you do not have a cookie press, make "dollars" instead of straws. Divide the dough in half and roll each half into a 1½-inch-thick log. Wrap dough in plastic and refrigerate for at least 1 hour. Slice into ¼-inch-thick rounds and arrange on baking sheet, leaving 1 inch between rounds. Bake as directed above.

MAMA'S WHIPPED CREAM POUND CAKE
Page 128

7

DESSERTS & BEVERAGES

I love dessert! Crunchy sweet, tart sweet, creamy sweet…just plain gooey sweet. It's all good, and I am happy to share some of my favorites with you. When you entertain, dessert should usually be the last thing on your mind, because you have prepared it in advance, and it waits patiently for presentation, right? Sometimes, like birthday cake or King Cake for your Mardi Gras party, dessert is the centerpiece on your sideboard, but often it is tucked away, waiting to be adored by your family and guests. When I was a child, dinner was the noon meal, and we had meat, vegetables, biscuits, cornbread and dessert every day. On Saturdays we all went to Gommey's house for dinner, where we dined in the same room that my father and his father's father had dinner many years before us. The desserts were wonderfully old-fashioned with liberal dollops of sweet whipped cream on nearly everything. Mmmmmmmmmm!

It's not every night that my family indulges in a homemade treat after supper, but I love to see the surprise in their eyes when I bring out Aunt Mary's Coconut Pie (page 132) or Mama's Whipped Cream Pound Cake (page 128) with Mama's Rum Sauce (page 130). Do not forget the whipped cream!

The beverage you pair with your meal can also make a statement—one that says, "You're in for a delightful experience." My Appletini (page 135) and Classic Southern Mimosa (page 136) recipes are great for special occasions and Sunday brunch.

MAMA'S WHIPPED CREAM POUND CAKE

1 cup butter, softened

3 cups sugar, sifted

3 cups cake flour, sifted

8 large eggs, room temperature

½ pint heavy cream

1 teaspoon vanilla extract

1 teaspoon almond extract

2 teaspoons brandy

Grease and flour a 10-inch tube pan or a 10-inch Bundt pan.

Using large bowl of mixer on high speed, cream butter until fluffy, approximately 10 minutes. Add sugar gradually, 2 tablespoons at a time, beating well after each addition.

Add ½ cup flour at a time and eggs (one egg at a time) alternately, beginning and ending with flour. Batter should be very smooth. Combine extracts and brandy with cream. Add cream mixture gradually, beating until well combined.

Pour batter into prepared pan, being careful not to spill batter on sides. Place pan on center rack in *cold oven*. Turn heat to 325°F and bake for 1 hour and 25 minutes. Do not open the oven door.

Remove cake to wire rack and cool in the pan for 15 minutes. Turn out onto rack to cool completely.

Yield: 1 large cake

Sister says: *This family recipe dates back to the early 1900s and is truly spectacular. Follow the instructions as given, even though the method seems strange to modern bakers. You must not open the oven door to check on your cake. If you must look, turn on the oven light for a quick peek through the glass. Did you know that when you turn on that light, a small new heat source begins, which can skew the shape of your cake? If you do look, remember to turn off the light afterward. Mama says not to fret if there is a small moist "sad streak" in the center; that's her favorite part!*

GREAT-GRANDMOTHER TEE'S FUDGE SAUCE

Using a double boiler or heavy saucepan over low heat, combine chocolate, salt, sugar, butter and corn syrup; cook, stirring constantly, until sugar melts completely.

Add boiling water and vanilla, stirring until well combined. Store in glass container at room temperature.

Yield: 1½ cups

2 squares bitter chocolate

½ teaspoon salt

1 cup sugar

4 tablespoons butter

2 tablespoons light corn syrup

¼ cup boiling water

2 teaspoons vanilla extract

Sister says:

Grandmother Tee's real name was Dorothy, and she was well-known for her splendid hospitality in Monroe, Louisiana. Many of her recipes are complicated, but this rich fudge sauce is easy to make and delicious. Serve it with ice cream or pound cake, but for a chocoholic like me, the possibilities are endless!

MAMA'S RUM SAUCE FOR POUND CAKE

½ cup butter

1 cup sugar

½ cup evaporated milk

2 teaspoons vanilla extract

2 teaspoons rum extract or 2 teaspoons dark rum

Sister says:

Mama says not to worry about storing leftovers; there won't be any!

Using a heavy saucepan over low heat, combine butter, sugar and evaporated milk, stirring until mixture is slightly thickened, approximately 3 to 5 minutes. Remove pan from heat.

Add vanilla and rum flavoring, stirring until well combined. Pour sauce into small pitcher and serve warm. Cover tightly and store in a glass container at room temperature for up to 24 hours.

Yield: 2 cups

CUSTARD FONDUE WITH TOASTED POUND CAKE

Using a double boiler over medium temperature, heat cream and milk, stirring occasionally, until mixture is almost boiling (small bubbles will form at sides of pan). Remove from heat. Using a medium bowl, whisk eggs with sugar briskly until mixture is light and well combined. Add ¼ cup of hot cream to egg mixture, whisking continuously. Pour egg mixture into cream and cook over medium-low heat, whisking constantly until mixture thickens, approximately 3 minutes. Do not boil.

Pour thickened custard into a glass bowl and cool. Cover tightly and refrigerate until ready to use. Allow custard to return to room temperature before serving.

Preheat oven to 425°F.

Line a rimmed baking pan with parchment paper.

Cut pound cake into 1-inch slices and lightly butter one side. Cut slices into 1-inch cubes. Arrange cake cubes on baking pan with space around each piece. Toast cake cubes, turning to toast reverse sides.

Place serving bowl with custard in center of serving tray and arrange toasted pound cake around bowl. Provide skewers or fondue forks. Garnish with edible flowers or rose petals.

½ cup heavy cream

1 cup whole milk

8 large egg yolks

½ cup sugar

1 teaspoon vanilla

Pound cake

Butter

Edible flowers or rose petals

Sister says: Use your favorite pound cake recipe, or try mine on page 128. Almost every lady in Gommey's day had a jealously guarded pound cake recipe. They rarely shared these treasured "receipts," quietly competing with each other at church socials to see who made the most beautiful and the most delicious cake. Remember, in those days, ovens had 3 temperatures: hot, medium or slow, and without air conditioning, humidity played a big part in baking success. (Humidity is still important to baking, but now we can control it to suit our needs.) This is one of my favorite desserts from our regular Saturday dinners at Gommey's house. I hope you like it, too.

AUNT MARY'S COCONUT PIE

1 deep-dish premium pie shell, thawed

¾ cup sugar

3 tablespoons cornstarch

¼ teaspoon salt

1 (12-ounce) can evaporated milk

6 ounces whole milk

3 egg yolks

2 tablespoons butter

1 teaspoon vanilla

1⅓ cups sweetened shredded coconut

½ pint heavy cream

2 tablespoons powdered sugar

1 teaspoon vanilla extract

Prick sides of pie shell and bake according to package directions. Cool and set aside.

Using a heavy saucepan over medium-low heat, combine sugar, cornstarch, evaporated milk, and milk, stirring constantly until slightly thick. Do not boil.

Whisk egg yolks until thick and lemon colored. Add 1 tablespoon of hot milk mixture to yolks, whisking to combine well. Pour egg yolk mixture into warm milk mixture; cook over low heat for 2 minutes, whisking constantly.

Remove from heat and add butter, vanilla and coconut, stirring until well combined. Let filling stand for 5 minutes.

Preheat oven to 350°F.

Pour filling into prepared pie shell and bake for 15 minutes. Cool pie on wire rack.

Sprinkle a few tablespoons of coconut on a lightly greased baking sheet and toast until light brown. Watch carefully; this only takes a minute. Remove from oven and set aside.

Just before serving, prepare sweetened whipped cream: Using medium bowl of mixer on high speed, whip cream with powdered sugar and vanilla until soft peaks form. Garnish pie with whipped cream topped with a generous sprinkling of toasted coconut.

Yield: 1 pie

This recipe is easily doubled.

LEMON-BLUEBERRY TRIFLE

2 pints blueberries, washed and sorted

2 pints strawberries, washed, hulled and cut into bite-sized pieces

Juice of 1 lemon plus 1 tablespoon of grated lemon rind

⅔ cup sugar, divided

2 teaspoons cornstarch

1 quart heavy cream

½ teaspoon almond extract

1 (11-ounce) jar lemon curd

1 pan Sister Schubert's Blueberry Rolls, prepared per package directions

Combine berries in a large bowl; sprinkle with ⅓ cup sugar, lemon juice, lemon rind and cornstarch. Using a large saucepan over medium heat, simmer berry mixture until berries begin to soften and release juice, approximately 3 minutes. Set aside to cool.

Using large bowl of mixer on high speed, whip cream with ⅓ cup sugar and almond extract until soft peaks form. Do not overbeat. Using a small bowl, combine a tablespoon of lemon curd with 2 tablespoons of whipped cream, stirring until well combined. Add remaining lemon curd and combine with whipped cream. Beat on high speed until somewhat stiffer peaks form and lemon curd is well combined.

Remove Blueberry Rolls from pan and cut into 1-inch pieces.

To Assemble:
Spoon a layer of whipped cream filling into a large glass trifle bowl. Add a layer of Blueberry Rolls. Add a layer of berries with juice. Continue layering until you have used all of the roll pieces and berries with juice. Finish with a layer of filling. Cover tightly and refrigerate until ready to serve.

Yield: 1 large trifle

Sister says:

My family loves this creamy rich dessert. You may use a china bowl, but then you'll miss the gorgeous colors of the berries with the soft white filling and dark purple Blueberry Rolls. You will bring a little taste of summer to your table any time you serve it!

WHITE CHOCOLATE BANANA ROLL PUDDING

4 large eggs, lightly beaten

1¼ cups light brown sugar, firmly packed, divided

4 cups half-and-half

1 teaspoon vanilla extract

8 ounces white chocolate morsels

1 package Sister Schubert's Clover Leaf Rolls, cut into bite-sized pieces

4 tablespoons butter

2 ripe bananas, peeled and cut into ½-inch dice

2 teaspoons sugar mixed with ½ teaspoon cinnamon

Preheat oven to 350°F.

Butter a 9 x 13-inch baking dish.

Using a large bowl, combine eggs, 1 cup brown sugar, half-and-half and vanilla, stirring until well combined. Add chocolate morsels and roll pieces, stirring until bread is completely wet.

Melt butter in small sauté pan; add ¼ cup brown sugar and bananas; cook over medium heat until sugar melts, approximately 2 minutes. Remove from heat. Stir sautéed bananas into custard mixture and pour into baking dish. Sprinkle with cinnamon sugar.

Bake until pudding is golden and center is set, approximately 1 hour. If the pudding begins to brown after 40 minutes, shield top with foil and continue baking. Serve warm with vanilla ice cream and chocolate sauce.

Yield: 6 to 8 servings

CLASSIC BLOODY MARY

Using a large pitcher, combine tomato juice, vodka, juice of 2 lemons, horseradish and Worcestershire sauce. Add hot pepper sauce to taste and stir to combine. Refrigerate for 4 hours, or overnight. To serve, add several ice cubes to each glass, and sprinkle with freshly ground black pepper and celery salt. Pour mixture into prepared glasses and garnish with celery stalks and lemon slices.

Yield: 4 to 6 servings

4 cups premium tomato juice

1 cup premium vodka

3 lemons (2 juiced, 1 sliced into rounds for garnish)

1 tablespoon prepared horseradish

2 tablespoons Worcestershire sauce

Hot pepper sauce to taste

Freshly ground black pepper

Celery salt

4 celery stalks with tops, washed and dried with a paper towel

Sister says: You might like to garnish your Bloody Mary with jalapeno-stuffed Spanish olives, or a swizzle skewer of baby artichoke hearts and olives. Get festive!

THE BEST APPLETINI

For each portion, fill a cocktail shaker with ice and add 2 ounces vodka and 2 ounces sour apple liqueur. Close tightly and shake vigorously for 30 seconds to 1 minute. Strain into frozen martini glass and garnish with apple slice.

4 martini glasses, frozen

Premium vodka

Sour apple liqueur

1 red or green apple, sliced crosswise

CLASSIC SOUTHERN MIMOSA

Champagne, chilled

Premium orange juice, chilled

Grand Marnier

Pour 2 ounces of orange juice into each champagne flute. Add 1 teaspoon Grand Marnier and stir. Carefully pour champagne down the side of the flute to fill three-quarters full.

Sister says: Champagne is such a festive way to start the day! Everyone has a favorite brand, but for this drink, buy semi-sec or slightly sweet champagne. Champagne flutes are too small for fruit garnish, but if you are using larger wine glasses, I like to garnish with an orange slice or a few ripe raspberries. You may pour the orange juice and Grand Marnier into your glasses ahead of time, but add the champagne just before serving.

BELLINI

Prosecco (Italian sparkling wine), chilled

Peach nectar, chilled

Peach schnapps, chilled

For each cocktail: Stir 1 ounce peach nectar and 1 ounce peach schnapps together in champagne flute. Gently pour Prosecco down the side to fill flute three-quarters full.

Sister says: Originally made with crushed white peaches, the delightful Bellini was invented at Harry's Bar in Venice. If you can find them, by all means, add crushed white peaches to your mix. You may substitute any champagne or Asti Spumante for Italian Prosecco, but I recommend the original. Thanks, Harry!

SISTER'S COFFEE PUNCH

2 quarts strong coffee

1 pint heavy cream

4 tablespoons sugar

1 tablespoon vanilla

1 quart premium vanilla ice cream

The day before your brunch, spoon softened ice cream into a ring mold, cover tightly and return to freezer. Brew strong coffee, cover tightly and refrigerate.

To serve, beat cream with sugar and vanilla into soft peaks. Add cold coffee and whisk to combine. Wrap ice mold with warm towel to release, and invert into punch bowl. Pour coffee mixture over and serve.

Yield: 25 to 30 servings

Sister says:

This venerable recipe is easily doubled for larger parties. Remember that the ingredients dictate the quality of the recipe, so use premium ice cream and coffee for best results. At the bakery and at home, I never skimp on the quality of the ingredients; this is the cornerstone of my success in the kitchen!

HOT CROSS BUNS
Page 152

8
HOLIDAY FAVORITES

Who doesn't love holiday food? Oftentimes, we wait all year for that one special dish. I am sure that your family has time-honored recipes that are served ceremoniously on holidays. Thanksgiving and Christmas have always been the most traditional in our family, with certain dishes that absolutely must be served: turkey and cornbread dressing, sweet potatoes, cranberry sauce, and of course, my rolls. I also like to introduce a new dish each year; sometimes it will replace an old favorite, and other times the family just cannot accept the change! A few years ago, I introduced the Cranberry Conserve recipe (page 140), and it has since become a family favorite. Success!

The hectic days between Thanksgiving and Christmas are filled with excitement and anticipation. With so many demands on our time, we must prioritize and focus. We cannot attend every holiday party and then expect to have the time we desire with family and friends. I try to remember what is important to my family and allow plenty of time for those special traditions. I always trim my kitchen for Christmas; it sets the tone and brings holiday cheer to the heart of my home. Baking and decorating cookies with my children and preparing beautiful breads for friends and family are just a few of the traditions I look forward to every year.

Whether your family gets together for Thanksgiving, Rosh Hashanah, Christmas, Mardi Gras, or Easter, there are recipes here that are sure to become holiday favorites. Don't be afraid to try something new. Focus on family and friends, and soon you will be creating holiday traditions that will continue for generations in your family.

CRANBERRY CONSERVE

1 orange

1¾ cups water

3 cups fresh cranberries, washed and sorted

1⅓ cups sugar

½ teaspoon ground cinnamon

¼ teaspoon ground cloves

1 firm Granny Smith apple

Squeeze juice from the orange and set aside. Scrape and discard orange pulp; cut rind into small dice. Using a small saucepan over high heat, combine orange rind and water; bring to a boil. Cook for 10 minutes, stirring occasionally; drain and reserve.

Using a medium saucepan over low heat, combine orange juice, orange rind, cranberries, sugar, cinnamon and cloves. Peel, core and quarter apple; cut into ½-inch dice and add to cranberry mixture. Bring to a boil over high heat; reduce heat and cover saucepan partially to allow steam to escape. Simmer over low heat, stirring occasionally, until mixture thickens, apples are tender and cranberries have burst, approximately 10 to 15 minutes.

Pour conserve into a glass serving dish and allow to cool for 1 hour. To store, cover tightly and refrigerate. Bring to room temperature before serving.

Yield: 4 cups

CRANBERRY BREAD

Preheat oven to 350°F.

Grease and flour a 9 x 5 x 3-inch loaf pan. Set prepared pan aside.

Combine chopped cranberries and sugar in a medium bowl. Grate rind from orange using large eyes of grater, being careful not to grate the white pith. Cut orange in half, and extract juice. Combine grated rind, juice, and melted butter in a 1-cup liquid measuring cup; add enough boiling water to orange juice mixture to equal 1 cup. Add orange juice mixture to cranberry mixture; let cool slightly. Add egg, stirring until well combined.

Combine flour and next 3 ingredients in a large bowl. Add cranberry mixture, stirring just until dry ingredients are moistened. Fold in pecans.

Pour batter into prepared pan. Bake for 1 hour or until a wooden pick inserted in center of loaf comes out clean. Cool in pan on a wire rack for 10 minutes. Turn out onto a wire rack, and cool completely.

Yield: 1 loaf

Note: This recipe is easily doubled.

1 cup fresh cranberries, coarsely chopped

1⅓ cups sugar

1 large orange

2 tablespoons butter, melted

About ½ cup boiling water

1 large egg, lightly beaten

2 cups all-purpose flour

1½ teaspoons baking powder

½ teaspoon baking soda

½ teaspoon salt

1 cup pecans, chopped

Sister says: This beautiful Cranberry Bread makes a thoughtful hostess gift for the holidays. If you use foil mini-loaf pans, bake for only 40 to 45 minutes, cool as directed above, and return cooled loaves to pans for gift wrapping.

SWEET POTATOES "BREARD"

3 cups baked sweet potato, peeled and mashed

1 cup sugar

3 large eggs, well beaten

1 tablespoon bourbon or 1 teaspoon vanilla extract

½ cup sweetened condensed milk

½ cup butter (1 stick), softened

Topping:

⅓ cup cold butter, chopped

⅓ cup all-purpose flour

1 cup light brown sugar

1 cup pecans, coarsely chopped

Preheat oven to 350°F.

Butter a 9 x 13-inch casserole.

Using large bowl of mixer, combine sweet potato, sugar, eggs, bourbon, condensed milk and butter. Mix on medium-high until well combined and smooth. Pour sweet potato mixture into prepared casserole.

Using a pastry blender (or two knives), chop butter, flour and sugar into the consistency of dry oatmeal. Sprinkle evenly over the sweet potato mixture, followed by the pecans.

Bake until brown and puffy, approximately 35 to 40 minutes.

Yield: 8 servings

Sister says: "Breard," a French surname from my mother's family, reminds me of happy days with my Grandmother Satchie from Monroe, Louisiana where Mama grew up. This is one of my grandmother's favorite recipes. A fixture at our Thanksgiving table for as long as I can remember, this simple but sophisticated dish has the lightness of a soufflé and a memorable flavor. I usually make a smaller dish topped with marshmallows (added the last 10 minutes of baking) for the children. Either way, even folks who don't like sweet potatoes love this version!

SWEET POTATO PIE

Preheat oven to 350°F.

Using a large mixing bowl, beat cooked sweet potatoes on medium speed with butter until smooth. Add eggs, beating continuously until well combined. Add sugar, milk, nutmeg and vanilla, beating well. Divide mixture into 2 piecrusts and sprinkle with orange zest. (You may bake the pies plain, or add Brown Sugar Topping.)

Chop sugar, flour and butter with a pastry blender or two knives, until topping resembles coarse crumbs. Fold in pecans and sprinkle evenly over pie mixture.

Bake on middle oven rack until center is set, approximately 45 to 50 minutes.

Yield: 12 servings

Note: This recipe may be halved.

Sister says: Sweet potatoes with a smooth outer surface usually have smoother insides as well! Choose medium potatoes with unblemished skin. We are blessed to have an abundant pecan crop in Alabama, and I love to cook with them. Remember to pick over your pecans carefully to remove any bitter shell remnants.

2 pounds sweet potatoes, prepared as directed*

½ cup butter, softened

3 large eggs

1 cup sugar

½ cup sweetened condensed milk

½ cup evaporated milk

1 teaspoon ground nutmeg

1 teaspoon vanilla extract

2 frozen deep-dish piecrusts, thawed

Zest from 1 medium orange

Brown Sugar Topping:

1 cup dark brown sugar

½ cup all-purpose flour

½ cup cold butter, chopped into pea-sized pieces

1 cup pecans, coarsely chopped

*Sweet potatoes may be baked until tender, or peeled, sliced and boiled for approximately 30 minutes until tender.

BROWN SUGAR SPREAD FOR HAM SANDWICHES

RAISIN SAUCE FOR SPIRAL-SLICED HAM

Using a double boiler over medium heat, combine sugar and cornstarch, stirring constantly until well blended and slightly thickened. Add remaining ingredients, stirring constantly until sauce is thick and fragrant. Serve warm.

Yield: 1½ cups

Note: Refrigerate leftover sauce.

½ cup dark brown sugar

1 tablespoon cornstarch

¼ cup red wine vinegar

1 cup port wine

½ cup golden raisins

½ teaspoon allspice

1 teaspoon dry mustard

Sister says: Any local grocery store will have a variety of spiral-sliced hams available. Again, I remind you to choose premium brands as this will help to ensure the best quality. Most of these hams come with a prepared sauce but I like to use my own. Let the fresh homemade flavor be your signature on a delicious spiral-sliced ham.

BROWN SUGAR SPREAD FOR HAM SANDWICHES

Mix ingredients in a small bowl, blending thoroughly. Cover tightly and refrigerate any leftover spread. This recipe is easily doubled or tripled.

4 tablespoons butter, softened

¾ cup light brown sugar, packed firmly

Pinch of ground cloves

Sister says: These easy sauces definitely fall into the category of "gilding the lily," and I am happy to share them with you!

PUMPKIN MOUSSE

Crust:

1½ cups crushed graham crackers (14 crackers)

½ cup light brown sugar

½ cup butter (1 stick), softened

Mousse:

½ cup half-and-half

1 (18 ounce) can pumpkin puree

1 cup dark brown sugar

¾ teaspoon salt

½ teaspoon ground cinnamon

¼ teaspoon ground nutmeg

¾ cup egg yolk (8–9 large eggs), stirred lightly

1 (¼-ounce) package gelatin, softened in ¼ cup water

1 ripe banana, mashed

1 pint heavy cream

1 teaspoon vanilla extract

2 tablespoons confectioner's sugar

Zest from 1 orange

For the crust: Combine all ingredients and spread into 9-inch tart (or pie) pan. (Use a measuring cup to press crumb mixture evenly.) Refrigerate crust.

For the mousse: Using a medium saucepan over medium heat, combine half-and-half, pumpkin, brown sugar, salt, cinnamon and nutmeg, stirring until well mixed. Add egg yolk slowly, stirring well after each addition. Add gelatin and banana, stirring until completely combined. Remove from heat and set aside until cool. Pour mousse into prepared graham cracker crust and smooth top. Cover and refrigerate until ready to serve.

Prepare whipped cream: Using a medium bowl, whisk cream with sugar and vanilla until soft peaks form when you lift the whisk.

Yield: 5 servings

To serve, garnish each slice of mousse with a generous dollop of whipped cream and a sprinkle of orange zest.

Sister says: *Hand-whipped cream is a simple and satisfying culinary skill. For best results, place your mixing bowl and whisk in the freezer 30 minutes before use. Use cold heavy cream and whisk briskly, scraping the sides of the bowl with each pass. In no time, you will have perfect whipped cream. We serve this rich sweet cream over fresh fruit, pies and lots of other sweet things. It's a Southern essential!*

TURKEY STUFFED SHELLS WITH BACON MARINARA SAUCE

Boil pasta in lightly salted water with 1 teaspoon oil, according to package directions for al dente, approximately 8 to 12 minutes. Drain and set aside.

Using a large skillet, sauté onion and garlic in olive oil until transparent. Add chopped artichoke hearts and turkey, tossing until heated through. Season with salt and pepper to taste and set aside until cool. Combine ricotta, egg, grated Parmesan and basil and add to turkey mixture.

Bacon Marinara Sauce:

6 pieces bacon
1 clove garlic, minced
1 (25-ounce) jar premium marinara sauce
½ to 1 teaspoon red pepper flakes

Fry bacon with garlic until crisp. Drain grease from pan and add marinara sauce and red pepper flakes, stirring to combine. Crumble bacon and reserve. Cook sauce over low heat until heated through. Set aside.

Preheat oven to 400°F.

Butter a 9 x 13-inch casserole.

Spread half of sauce in prepared casserole. Carefully spoon turkey mixture into cooked shells and arrange on marinara sauce. Drizzle remaining sauce over stuffed shells and top with mozzarella cheese. Sprinkle crumbled bacon over cheese.

Bake until cheese is beginning to brown and sauce is bubbly, approximately 25 to 30 minutes.

Yield: 6 servings

---

1 package large pasta shells (for stuffing)

¼ cup extra-virgin olive oil

½ medium onion, finely chopped

3 cloves garlic, minced

1 (14-ounce) can premium artichoke hearts, drained, chopped

2 cups cooked turkey, chopped

Salt and pepper

1 cup ricotta cheese

1 large egg, beaten

½ cup Parmesan cheese, grated

1 sprig fresh basil, chopped

2 cups mozzarella cheese, grated

KING CAKE FOR MARDI GRAS

1 package active dry yeast

2 tablespoons warm water (110°F to 115°F)

1 teaspoon salt

2 tablespoons sugar

¼ cup whole milk

3 teaspoons orange zest, finely chopped

2 cups all-purpose flour

1 teaspoon ground cinnamon

2 eggs, lightly beaten

¾ cup butter, cold

Small plastic baby (or a red kidney bean)

Egg Wash:

1 egg, lightly beaten

2 tablespoons water

Pecan Filling:

1 cup pecan pieces, roasted until fragrant

⅔ cup light brown sugar, firmly packed

1 teaspoon vanilla extract

½ teaspoon ground allspice

Dash salt

4 tablespoons maple syrup

Dissolve yeast in warm water in the large bowl of a stand mixer fitted with dough hook; let stand 5 to 10 minutes until frothy.

Combine salt, sugar, orange zest and milk in a small bowl. Combine milk mixture with yeast mixture. Combine cinnamon and flour in a separate bowl.

With mixer on low speed, alternate adding flour and beaten eggs a little at a time, beginning and ending with flour, until completely incorporated. Knead on low speed for 10 minutes. Dough will be smooth and elastic. Chop cold butter into small pieces; with mixer at low speed, add butter slowly until incorporated. Do not melt butter.

Place dough into a well-oiled bowl and turn to coat top. Cover loosely with a damp tea towel and allow to rise in a warm place (85°F), free from drafts, for 1 hour or until dough has doubled in bulk. Punch down, cover with plastic wrap and refrigerate for 8 hours or overnight.

Prepare filling: Combine all ingredients, stirring until well blended.

Remove dough from refrigerator and allow to return to room temperature. Roll dough out on a lightly floured surface to a 6 x18-inch rectangle. Spread pecan filling over surface of dough, leaving a 1½-inch margin on each side. Place the plastic baby (or kidney bean) somewhere in the filling.

Fold long side of dough over and roll tightly. Place the dough roll on a lightly greased baking sheet and form into a circle, seam side down, tucking one end into the other. With wet fingertips, seal the seam. Cover loosely with a damp tea towel and allow to rise in a warm place, free from drafts, until doubled in bulk, for approximately 45 minutes.

Preheat oven to 350°F.

Prepare egg wash: beat egg and 2 tablespoons water until well combined. Brush over surface of dough.

Bake until golden brown and bread sounds hollow when tapped, approximately 30 to 35 minutes. Remove to wire rack to cool.

Prepare glaze: Combine powdered sugar, almond extract and milk, stirring until glaze is a smooth fluid consistency. Divide between 3 small bowls; tint one batch purple, one green and one yellow, stirring until well combined. Place tinted glaze into 3 small zipper bags and seal, pressing air out. Snip one corner of each bag and drizzle over cooled bread. (Traditionally, the colors are applied to separate sections, but use your creativity here.)

Decorate the platter with doubloons and Mardi Gras beads.

Yield: 1 large loaf

Glaze:

1 cup powdered sugar

¼ teaspoon almond extract

1–2 tablespoons milk

Green, purple, and yellow paste food coloring

Sister says:

King Cake is prepared to celebrate the arrival of the three wise men (kings), bearing gifts for the baby Jesus twelve days after Christmas, which is known as the Feast of the Epiphany, Twelfth Night or King's Day. The round shape symbolizes the circuitous route they took in order to confuse King Herod, and the colors represent justice (purple), faith (green) and power (gold). A figurine symbolizing the baby Jesus may be baked inside, and the lucky person who finds it must host the next King's Day party. Make certain to tell your guests about the baby; a broken tooth is not lucky!

MAMIE'S CORNBREAD DRESSING

2 cups celery, finely chopped

2 cups bell pepper, finely chopped

½ cup onion, finely chopped

2 tablespoons butter

2 pans Sister Schubert's Southern Cornbread, baked

4 cups fresh turkey broth

1 cup butter (2 sticks), melted

2 tablespoons fresh thyme, finely chopped

2 tablespoons fresh sage, finely chopped

2 tablespoons fresh parsley, finely chopped

Salt and pepper

5 medium or 6 large eggs, beaten well

Preheat oven to 350°F.

Prepare two well-buttered 9 x 13-inch casseroles.

Sauté celery, bell pepper and onion in 2 tablespoons butter until tender. Crumble cornbread into a large mixing bowl and add sautéed vegetables, turkey broth, melted butter and herbs, stirring until ingredients are well combined. Blend in beaten eggs. (Batter will have a wet consistency.)

Divide batter into prepared pans and bake until golden brown, approximately 55 to 60 minutes. The tried-and-true cake test works for this dressing as well: when it's done, a wooden pick inserted into the center comes out clean.

Yield: 10 to 15 servings

Note: For fewer servings, this recipe may be reduced by half.

Sister says: We have this dressing at Thanksgiving and again at Christmas, but it's delicious no matter when you serve it. If you make the dressing ahead of time and do not have fresh turkey broth, chicken broth is an acceptable substitute. If you use chicken broth, remember to drizzle a little of your hot turkey broth over the dressing just before serving. Use two large pans instead of one giant pan; the dressing will be evenly baked with a rich crust.

MAMIE'S CORNBREAD DRESSING

HOT CROSS BUNS

1 cup milk

½ cup shortening

1½ packages active dry yeast

¾ cup warm water (105°F to 115°F)

½ teaspoon sugar

5 cups all-purpose flour, divided

⅓ cup sugar

1 teaspoon salt

½ teaspoon ground cardamom

3 large eggs

1 cup golden raisins

½ cup dried apricots, coarsely chopped

½ teaspoon vanilla extract

1 cup sifted powdered sugar

1 tablespoon plus 1 teaspoon milk

¼ teaspoon almond extract

¼ teaspoon vanilla extract

Combine 1 cup milk and shortening in a saucepan; heat until shortening melts, stirring occasionally. Cool to 105°F to 115°F.

Combine yeast, warm water, and ½ teaspoon sugar in a 2-cup liquid measuring cup; let stand 5 minutes. Combine milk mixture and yeast mixture.

Combine 2 cups flour, ⅓ cup sugar, salt, and cardamom in a large bowl. Add yeast mixture, stirring vigorously until well blended. Add eggs, one at a time, stirring well after each addition. Stir in raisins, apricots and ½ teaspoon vanilla. Stir in remaining 3 cups flour, 1 cup at a time, stirring vigorously until dough pulls away from sides of bowl.

Turn dough out onto a well-floured surface, and knead lightly until smooth and elastic (about 10 minutes). Place dough in a well-greased bowl, turning to coat top. Cover loosely, and let rise in a warm place (85°F), free from drafts, for 45 minutes or until doubled in bulk.

Turn dough out onto a lightly floured surface. Divide dough into 16 equal portions. Shape each portion into a ball. Place on 2 large greased baking sheets, leaving 2 inches of space between rolls. Cover loosely with damp tea towels, and let rise in a warm place, free from drafts, for 30 to 45 minutes or until doubled in bulk.

Preheat oven to 375°F.

Bake for 13 to 15 minutes, or until rolls are golden brown. Remove rolls from baking sheets and cool on wire racks.

Combine powdered sugar and remaining 3 ingredients; stir vigorously until icing is smooth and slightly stiff. The icing should be thick enough to hold its shape when piped. If too thin, add powdered sugar and beat well. If too thick, add milk by droplets, beating until reaching desired consistency. Spoon icing into small zipper bag and seal. Snip a tiny hole in one corner of bag. Pipe icing over top of each bun to form an "x." Allow icing to set before serving.

Yield: 16 buns

Sister says: These slightly sweet old-fashioned buns are traditionally baked for Good Friday.

TIPSY EGGNOG BREAD

2½ cups all-purpose flour

2 teaspoons baking powder

1 teaspoon salt

¼ teaspoon ground nutmeg

¼ teaspoon ground cinnamon

2 large eggs

1¼ cups premium eggnog

1 cup sugar

½ cup butter, melted

2 teaspoons bourbon

1 teaspoon vanilla extract

Preheat oven to 350°F.

Grease the bottom only of a 9 x 5 x 3-inch loaf pan. Set prepared pan aside.

Sift first 5 ingredients together. Set aside. Beat eggs in a large mixing bowl at medium-high speed in an electric mixer until light and frothy. Add eggnog and remaining 4 ingredients, beating at medium speed until well blended.

Add flour mixture to eggnog mixture, ½ cup at a time, stirring just until dry ingredients are moistened after each addition.

Pour batter into prepared pan. Bake for 45 to 50 minutes or until a wooden pick inserted in center comes out clean. Cool loaf in pan on a wire rack for 10 minutes; remove from pan and allow loaf to cool completely on a wire rack.

Yield: 1 loaf

Sister says:

If you don't plan to enjoy this bread right away, wrap tightly and refrigerate for up to 2 days.

EASTER BREAD

½ cup plus 2 tablespoons milk, divided

½ cup butter

1½ packages active dry yeast

½ cup warm water (105°F to 115°F)

¾ cup plus 1 teaspoon sugar, divided

4½ cups all-purpose flour, divided

1 tablespoon grated lemon rind

1½ teaspoons salt

1 teaspoon vanilla extract

¾ teaspoon almond extract, divided

3 large eggs, lightly beaten

1 cup powdered sugar, sifted

½ cup blanched slivered almonds, lightly toasted

Combine ½ cup milk and butter in a saucepan; heat until butter melts. Cool to 105°F to 115°F. Combine yeast, warm water, and 1 teaspoon sugar in a 1-cup liquid measuring cup; let stand 5 minutes. Combine milk mixture and yeast mixture.

Combine remaining ¾ cup sugar, 2 cups flour, lemon rind, and salt in a large bowl. Stir in yeast mixture, vanilla, and ½ teaspoon almond extract. Add eggs; stir vigorously for 2 minutes. Add remaining 2½ cups flour; stir until dough pulls away from bowl. Place dough in a well-greased bowl, turning to grease top. Cover loosely with a damp tea towel, and let rise in a warm place (85°F), free from drafts, for 1½ hours or until doubled in bulk.

Punch dough down; turn out onto floured surface. Shape into a 10-inch round; place in a greased 10-inch springform pan. Cover loosely with a damp tea towel; let rise in a warm place, free from drafts, for 1 hour or until doubled in bulk.

Preheat oven to 350°F.

Bake for 50 to 55 minutes or until golden brown. Remove from pan, and allow to cool on a wire rack.

Place wax paper under wire rack. Combine powdered sugar, remaining 2 tablespoons milk, and remaining ¼ teaspoon almond extract; drizzle over bread. Sprinkle with almonds.

Yield: 1 loaf

Sister says: *This lovely Easter bread is a centerpiece at my Easter brunch. I like to place a small pot of tulips in the center of the loaf and artificial Easter grass around the base nestled with pastel Easter eggs.*

EASTER BREAD

SISTER'S CINNAMON BREAD PUDDING

1 pan Sister Schubert's Cinnamon Rolls

8 egg yolks

2 eggs

1 quart heavy cream

1 cup sugar

Pinch of salt

2 tablespoons butter, cut into small cubes

1 cup pecans, coarsely chopped

½ cup golden raisins

2 teaspoons bourbon or 1 teaspoon vanilla extract

Sister says:

For a more fragrant topping, soak raisins in a few tablespoons of bourbon until plump and rehydrated. The alcohol cooks out during baking, leaving the wonderful flavor behind. This bread pudding bakes up beautifully—golden brown on top, soft and rich inside and brimming with sweet cinnamon flavor.

Butter a 9 x 13-inch casserole dish.

Remove rolls from package, and cut into 1-inch cubes.

Using a large mixing bowl, whisk eggs with egg yolks until light and fluffy. Add cream, sugar and salt, whisking to combine thoroughly. Flavor custard with bourbon or vanilla extract, stirring until well distributed.

Place rolls into prepared casserole and pour custard over. Make certain that all of the bread is wet with custard. Dot casserole with butter and sprinkle with pecans and raisins. Cover tightly and refrigerate for 8 hours or overnight.

Preheat oven to 350°F.

Bake on center rack until pudding is golden and center is set, approximately 55 to 60 minutes. Allow pudding to stand for 10 minutes before serving.

Yield: 6 to 8 servings

CHRISTMAS SUGAR COOKIES

Combine flour, salt and baking powder in a medium bowl, stirring well. Using a large mixing bowl, cream butter with sugar on high speed until fluffy and light, approximately 5 minutes. Beat in egg, vanilla and almond extract. With mixer on low speed, add flour mixture slowly and beat until well combined. Divide dough in half and wrap each part in plastic wrap. Refrigerate for 30 minutes to an hour.

Preheat oven to 375°F.

Line a large baking sheet with parchment paper.

One at a time, roll dough out to ¼-inch thickness. Cut out cookies using your favorite cookie cutters. Transfer to baking sheet and bake 10 to 12 minutes. Cookies will be pale, not brown. Cool cookies on wire racks for 30 minutes.

Yield: 24 medium cookies

2 cups all-purpose flour

½ teaspoon salt

¼ teaspoon baking powder

¾ cup butter, softened

¾ cup sugar

1 large egg

½ teaspoon vanilla extract

½ teaspoon almond extract

Sister says: *Whatever you do, have fun with sugar cookies! I like to dip my cutters in flour to make sure they cut cleanly. Before baking, decorate with sugar or colored sprinkles, or wait until cookies are cool and ice with decorator icing. You don't need an expensive icing bag; just add icing to small zipper bags and cut one corner. Voilà! I see a cookie decorating party in your future!*

HOLIDAY STRUDEL

- 1 cup butter, softened
- ½ (8-ounce) package cream cheese, softened
- 1 cup sour cream
- 5 cups all-purpose flour
- 2 (13-ounce) jars cherry preserves, divided
- 2 cups powdered sugar, sifted
- ¼ cup milk
- ½ teaspoon vanilla extract
- 1 cup sliced almonds, lightly toasted
- 1 cup green candied cherries, quartered
- 1 cup red candied cherries, quartered

Beat butter and cream cheese at medium speed in an electric mixer until creamy, approximately 5 minutes. Add sour cream, beating until well blended. Add flour, 1 cup at a time, beating until dough pulls away from sides of bowl. Cover bowl tightly with plastic wrap, and chill for at least 2 hours (up to 8 hours).

Preheat oven to 350°F.

Turn dough out onto a floured surface; divide into 4 equal portions. Prepare one strudel at a time; keep remaining dough wrapped and chilled until ready to use.

For each strudel, roll one portion of dough into a 16 x 12-inch rectangle. Spread one-fourth of preserves to within 1 inch of edges.

Fold long sides of dough to meet in center, pressing edges to seal. Fold short sides of dough to meet in center, pressing edges to seal. Place strudel, seam side down, on one half of a large greased baking sheet. (You will be placing 2 strudels on each baking sheet.) Score strudel crosswise at 1-inch intervals using a sharp knife, cutting through top layer of dough to reveal preserves.

Bake for 45 minutes or until crust is golden and filling is bubbly. Remove strudels from baking sheets, and let cool on wire racks.

Place wax paper under wire racks. Combine powdered sugar, milk, and vanilla; stir until smooth. Drizzle mixture over strudels. Quickly, before icing dries, decorate with almonds and candied cherries. Cut into slices to serve.

Yield: 4 strudels

Sister says: Your family will love this holiday treat, and it makes a great gift for anyone on your list. Wrapped in red cellophane and beautifully beribboned, this is the ultimate holiday gift from your kitchen! If you would like to prepare only 2 strudels at a time, tightly wrap and chill the remaining portions of dough for up to 2 days. Tightly wrapped baked strudels freeze well for up to one month.

HOLIDAY STRUDEL

ALMOND CHRISTMAS BRAID

1 package active dry yeast

⅔ cup warm milk (105°F to 115°F)

2 tablespoons sugar

¼ cup butter, melted and divided

1 large egg, lightly beaten

2¼ cups all-purpose flour

1 tablespoon grated orange rind

½ teaspoon salt

1 cup powdered sugar, sifted

1 tablespoon milk

¼ teaspoon almond extract

½ cup blanched slivered almonds, toasted

Red and green candied cherries (optional)

Combine yeast and warm milk in a 2-cup liquid measuring cup; let stand 5 minutes. Stir in 2 tablespoons sugar, 2 tablespoons melted butter, and egg. Combine flour, orange rind, and salt in a large bowl. Add yeast mixture; stir well.

Turn dough out onto a well-floured surface; knead until smooth and elastic (7 to 9 minutes). Place in a well-greased bowl, turning to grease top. Cover loosely; let rise in a warm place (85°F), free from drafts, for 1 hour or until doubled in bulk.

Punch down dough; turn out onto a lightly floured surface. Divide into thirds. Roll each third into a 24-inch rope. Place ropes on a large greased baking sheet. Braid ropes; join ends of ropes, and shape braid into an oval. Brush loaf with remaining melted butter. Cover loosely with a damp tea towel; let rise in a warm place, free from drafts, for 45 minutes or until doubled in bulk.

Preheat oven to 350°F.

Bake for 35 to 40 minutes or until golden brown. Remove from baking sheet, and let cool on a wire rack.

Place wax paper under rack. Combine powdered sugar, 2 tablespoons milk, and almond extract; drizzle over braid. Sprinkle evenly with almonds. Decorate with candied cherries, if desired.

Yield: 1 large braided loaf

Sister says: It is simply beautiful; this wreathed loaf is delicious as well. The aroma of freshly baked yeast bread with almonds and oranges is heavenly.

Children in the Kitchen

Cooking with children may be a slightly challenging and time-consuming experience. It was not until I had children of my own that I realized how much love and patience my grandmother, mother, and aunts had for my siblings and me when we were in the kitchen. When my children were young, I might hesitate when I heard the words, "Can I help, Mommy?" I must admit that my first thought was, I could do this much quicker by myself; then I remembered Gommey's voice as she talked me through the baking process. I remembered her floured hands as she kneaded the dough. I am thankful for the foundation these remarkable women established in my life. I was fortunate to relive wonderful times in the kitchen with my own children and now with my grandchildren.

I have learned that it is okay to let them crack the eggs even if I have to fish out the shells, and I never worry when more flour ends up on the floor than in the bowl. The lessons, the laughter, and the love are the three most important ingredients of the day! When you bake with your children, you teach them an invaluable skill and create lasting memories. Memories are a curious thing. We tend to live our whole lives trying to recapture feelings from our youth that we remember as magical. Occasionally, a memory is fuzzy after only a few years, but sometimes the ones that are truly meaningful are as clear today as they were forty years ago. Look at the world around you through the eyes of a child, and you may rekindle some of your own happy memories.

Portraits left to right:
Sister's children and grandchildren; Mary Margaret, Anna, Alex, Thomas, and Clay

Cast you

Upon th

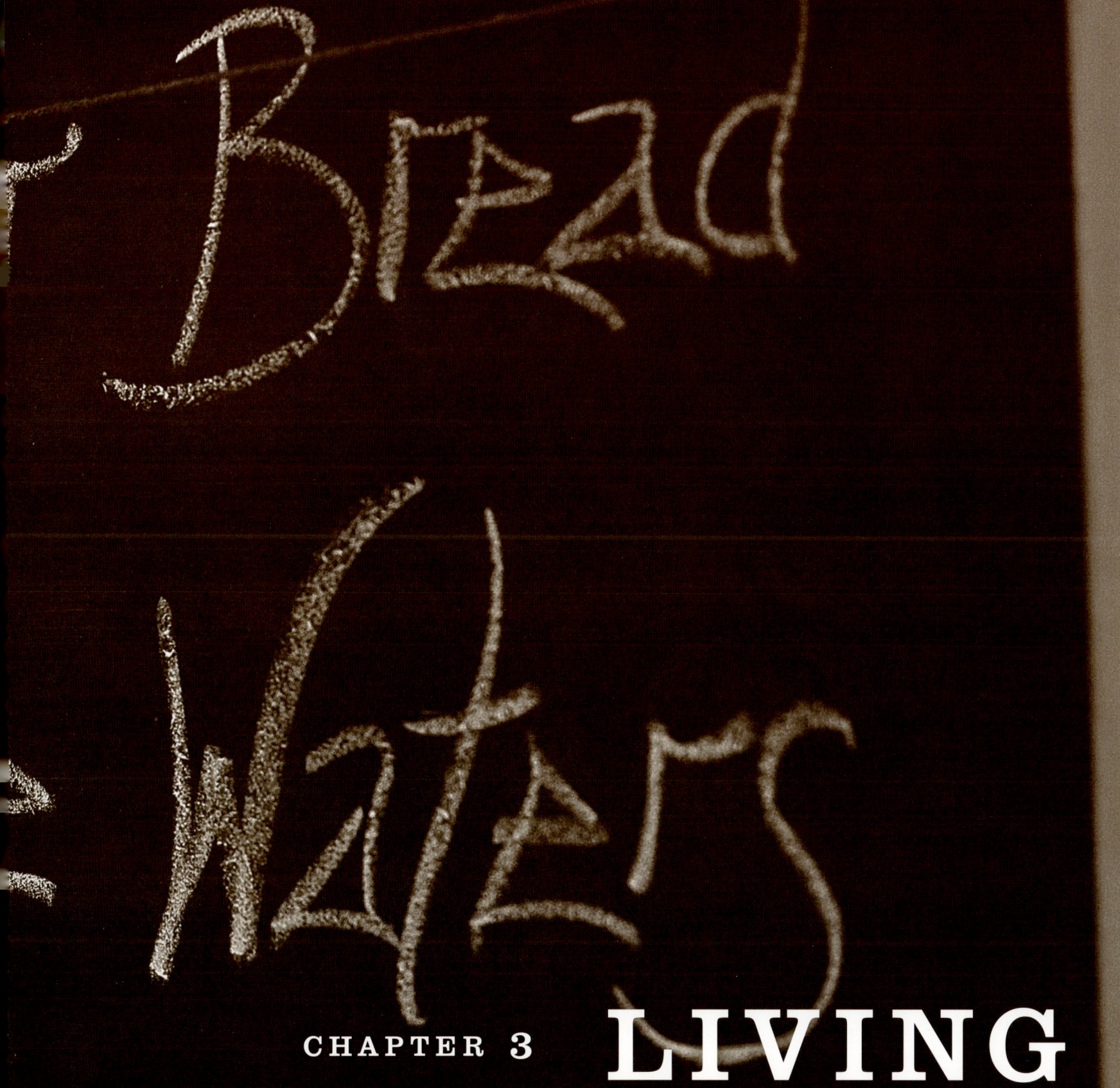

CHAPTER 3 **LIVING** Bread Waters

SOWING & REAPING *Success in Life's Work*

"Now he who supplies seed for the sower and bread for food will also supply and increase your store of seed and will enlarge the harvest of your righteousness. You will be made rich in every way so that you can be generous on every occasion."

—2 Corinthians 9:10

After we sold our stock in Sister Schubert's Homemade Rolls, my husband, George, and I decided that there was a greater purpose for our financial abundance. In 2001, we set up the Barnes Family Foundation, a 501(c)(3) charitable organization dedicated to improving the lives of the less fortunate and enhancing the community through education, historical preservation, and compassion. This current chapter in my life has been extraordinary. I have been busier than ever and continue to rely on my faith to guide me.

In 1991, I asked God to help me start my business, and I would help Him feed the hungry people of the world. In essence, I entered into a business partnership with my Lord, as I already had a personal relationship with Him. He has been my silent partner ever since, guiding me along the way.

The phenomenal growth of Sister Schubert's Homemade Rolls has taken me from my kitchen to the boardroom in a rather short time. George and I were financially blessed when we sold the stock in our company. We are very grateful to remain a part of the company that was started in my kitchen. I have a new calling now that does not involve baking, but it does involve food and a promise. God helped me start my business; now I must help Him feed the hungry people of the world.

Our Mission:

To show by what we do—that we are thankful for food in a hungry world, that we are thankful for friendship in a lonely world, but mostly, that we are thankful for the opportunity to help save and love all of God's children in the world.

Charity Begins at Home

Barnes Family Foundation believes that no one should go hungry. The foundation began its charitable giving by helping local food banks and area shelters in their efforts to feed the hungry. We continue to donate rolls and cash to charities and churches providing food to the needy. Anyone can donate to a food pantry, and, if you don't have the financial means, you can volunteer your services. Endless opportunities to help can be found in your own communities. Charitable organizations are always looking for volunteers to help. Check with your local town officials, and they will be able to direct you. Community service provides much-needed support to local organizations. I encourage everyone to get involved in their community and be *the difference you want to see in the world*.

Pictured left:
Sister with her sons and grandchildren

Pictured top right:
Mary Margaret, Thomas, and Anna

Pictured bottom right:
Sister with her daughter Chrissie

Helping Others

In an effort to make our young people aware of the world around them, the Barnes Family Foundation has established the Sister Schubert Annual Scholarship for Study Abroad. The goal of the scholarship is to expand the worldview of deserving students by introducing them to the peoples and cultures outside our country. We believe in educating our youth using a hands-on approach. This scholarship will give selected students an experience larger than themselves which they could not have afforded otherwise and an opportunity to help children and people outside the United States. Students may apply for this annual scholarship to study abroad through the Auburn University School of Human Sciences.

Inspiration is Contagious

I took my grandmother's recipe for *Everlasting Rolls* and turned it into my calling. I was inspired by Gommey's spirit, her talent, and her confidence in me. I encourage everyone to be that guiding force in others. Whatever you are doing, take time to think about how your actions might impact someone else. Sometimes, a simple word of praise is all someone needs to inspire them to continue their journey.

When I see a couple holding hands, I smile to myself. It makes me happy to see this sweet, simple gesture of love and friendship. Inspiration is all around us.

When I recall the times in my life that I have been inspired to try a new recipe, embark on an adventure, or step out of my comfort zone, I often wonder where that inspiration came from. Now I realize that these have not been moments of great discovery but, like the couple holding hands, moments of tiny gifts.

The book, *God's Dream*, by Archbishop Desmond Tutu and Douglas Carlton Adams, was a favorite bedtime story in our family. In this beautifully written tale, children learn to treat each other with compassion, understanding, and unity. The book emphasizes love, sharing, forgiveness, and seeing others the way God sees them. I had been taught this message since I was a child, but somehow, when I read it in this format to my own children, it was an inspiration—a reawakening—calling me to action.

I never saw myself as an international humanitarian worker, but after listening to a missionary talk about the forgotten children of Ukraine, I became one. The passion, commitment, and urgency in his voice stirred something inside me. His words were the inspiration I needed to act.

Couples holding hands, a bedtime story with my children, and the passion in a missionary's voice are only a few of the inspirations in my life. I hope that you will look for the subtle inspirations in your own life and appreciate that the majority of them are coming from interactions with other people.

Sasha's Home *Gorlovka, Ukraine*

"By wisdom a house is built, and through understanding it is established."
—Proverbs 24:3

In an effort to be the difference I wanted to see in the world, I focused on caring for God's children. I believe that the purity of youth is a gift that must be protected, and to that end, a loving family and a warm home have the ability to transform a child's life. My vision of Sasha's Home was realized through the dedication of so many people who shared our dream.

When opportunity knocks, you must open the door. That simple phrase is a wonderful reminder to always keep your eyes and hearts open to the possibilities. We all have busy lives and can get caught up in the day-to-day activities of work and family; yet that is no excuse to ignore the world around you. I know in my heart, when an opportunity presents itself, whether or not it is right for me. I believe that, through prayer and faith and external circumstances, God is able to use us where there is a need.

In 2001, a friend asked me to attend a local Rotary Club meeting. A missionary named Kenny Payne was scheduled to speak about his experience with abandoned children in Ukraine. I was busy working at the bakery in Luverne, and could think of a thousand other things I should be doing, but I listened to that quiet voice inside that whispered, "Go, this is an opportunity." Kenny spoke with such compassion, commitment, and urgency that I knew I would get involved at some level, but I never could have imagined how personal my involvement would become. Kenny and his wife, Lora, described firsthand the poverty and lack of assistance available to these innocent abandoned children. When they asked for financial assistance, I immediately pledged to help. With funds from the Barnes Family Foundation, we were able to send financial assistance, as well as flour, beans, and rice.

I know God led me to that Rotary meeting, but I also felt there was more I should be doing. I simply asked the Lord to let me know when it was time for me to do more. I told Him I would be listening. A few years later, in 2004, I accompanied Kenny and Lora to

LIVING 167

Alex was born with two clubbed feet. A nurse told me that, due to his impairment, Alex's chances of being adopted were slim and he would most likely spend his childhood days in a Ukrainian state-run institution. Not wanting to accept this prognosis, I made arrangements for Alex to travel to America for medical treatment. Of course, we fell in love with Alex and adopted him. When I watch Alex play baseball, it's almost hard to imagine that, not long ago, he was in foot braces. God is so good!

Gorlovka, Ukraine. While touring the Abandoned Baby Center, I saw so many children in need. The limited resources available in Ukraine are so meager that these children get barely enough to sustain themselves. With Kenny and Lora's tireless efforts, we were able to take over a wing of the hospital. We equipped the building with beds, toys, and caregivers, and supplied the children with enough formula, food, and love to allow them to flourish and thrive. We named it The Family Care Center.

When I least expected it, one freezing cold day at the Abandoned Baby Center, God introduced me to Alexsey, my future son. From the beginning, I knew it would be hard for me to resist these desperate babies, but suddenly, completely, I connected with 2-year-old Alexsey. There was something in his eyes, his smile, his fierce embrace; I know in my heart it was a divine introduction. Fourteen months after meeting him, our family welcomed Alex into his new home.

"Sasha" is the Russian nickname for Alexsey; with its warm, safe, and comforting tone, I thought it only fitting to name our new foster care facility "Sasha's Home." Through it, we are able to provide temporary and permanent homes for children who have been abandoned or orphaned. We believe that the nurture of a caring family will make all the difference in the lives of the children and adults we are able to help.

Progressing from an invitation to a Rotary Club meeting, to a trip to Ukraine, to adopting Alex, and then building a foster care center in a faraway land, all in a few short years, is truly an amazing feat. Completely humbled by the task before me, and always with God's help, I will continue this journey.

Get The Word Out

Change The World Fundraiser Event (clockwise):
Gina Shiflett with Sister; Caliza Pool in Alys Beach; kids enjoying synchronized swimmers

One thing I have noticed over the last few years is that there are so many people who want to help but they do not know where to begin. I am never shy when talking about the needs of my charities, and it has led to an abundance of blessings on more than one occasion. Don't be hesitant to talk to friends and family about the woman you know who needs a reliable car to get to work or the family who lost everything in a fire and needs a place to stay while they figure out "what now." I know this because a few years ago I sat in the chair at Salon Twist in Grayton Beach, Florida, and told my hair stylist, owner Gina Shiflett, about my desire to help the abandoned children of Ukraine. Somewhere between my shampoo, cut, and blow-dry, she was telling me about the charity event she started the year before called Change The World Fundraiser and that she wanted the Barnes Family Foundation to be the next year's recipient of the proceeds. She was so excited about helping me in this endeavor; she took on the challenge with gusto and had a real heart for my foundation.

On November 1, 2007, the 2nd Annual Change the World Fundraiser, held in beautiful Alys Beach, raised more than $100,000 to aid Ukrainian orphans in Sasha's Home. The outpouring of generosity and kindness was overwhelming. Donations of money and items for the silent auction were more than I could ever have imagined. Alys Beach, a stunning new resort town located on Florida's famous Scenic Highway 30A, donated the venue for the evening. With the beautiful Caliza Pool as our backdrop, we could not have been more blessed.

So remember: share your thoughts, ideas, dreams, and desires. Who knows? Maybe someone listening shares your passion.

Preserving History

If you don't know where you came from, how do you know where you're going and what you're supposed to be?

The Barnes Family Foundation strongly believes in preserving our heritage through maintaining and restoring historical sites. In an effort to save our history, the foundation has supported several restoration projects in Alabama, including the Pioneer Museum of Alabama in Troy, Alabama. The foundation provided artifacts and cash donations to assist this excellent museum of pioneer life and times in Alabama.

Most recently, the Barnes Family Foundation purchased the Henderson House in Troy, Alabama. The house originally belonged to members of my family and is listed in the National Historical Registry. The foundation guided the one-million-dollar renovation and restoration process, paying close attention to keeping true to the period of the house through cosmetic and architectural changes. In the summer of 2008, the handsome, sophisticated home was reopened to

the public. Jeremiah Augustus Henderson built the nearly 6,000-square-foot house for his wife, Millie Henderson, in 1867. Henderson constructed the home of wood lath with heart pine floors and magnificent moldings throughout. The Henderson family history is woven tightly into the history of their city and state. Their son, Charles Henderson, went on to become Governor of Alabama. He had no children, so upon his death, he bequeathed the bulk of his estate to a trust established to care for the children of Pike County. As a result, the Charles Henderson Middle School, Charles Henderson High School, and Charles Henderson Child Health Center were established in his memory.

The thread that connects us to the past wraps around us and goes on. We are connected, representatives of a continuing legacy from our ancestors, with a responsibility to remember, improve, and carry on. If you would like to know how you can help, or need more information on the Barnes Family Foundation, please visit our website at www.BarnesFamilyFoundation.org.

Sister's Achievements

Leon Loard Portrait Studios;
Painting by Shari Ford

2009 – "Alabama Citizen of the Year" by the Alabama Broadcasters Association for Sister's representation of Alabama to the United States

2009 – "International Humanitarian Award - Gorlov Medal" by the city of Gorlovka, Ukraine, for Sister's work in establishing Sasha's Home

2006 – "Most Inspiring Woman Over 50 Award" by The Kappa Delta Alumnae Association

2004 – Alabama Culinary Ambassador; appointment by Governor Riley

2004 – "The Outstanding Kappa Delta of the Year Award" by The Kappa Delta Alumnae Association (Only 5 KD alums in the country receive this award each year.)

2000 – "Large Manufacturing Industry Employer of the Year Award" by the Committee on Employment of People with Disabilities

2000 – "The Lowder Entrepreneur of the Year" by Colonial Bank

The Bread Of Life

Food, family, and faith are the themes that run through this book and through my life and business as well. I will never forget that I began Sister Schubert's Homemade Rolls by baking rolls as a fund-raiser for St. Mark's Episcopal Church in Troy, Alabama. I have progressed through many transitions since that time, but my heart always knows that my strength and creative energy come from God. Each time I faced a difficult challenge or a potential obstacle in my life, I looked to my faith for guidance. I did not always receive the answer I hoped for, but somehow I received the answer I needed.

If someone had told me, when I was making rolls on my sun porch, that one day soon I would be looking for a 25,000-square-foot building (and a few years after that, a 100,000-square-foot building) to meet the needs of our distributors, I would have laughed. How could I fathom such an enormous and overwhelming prospect? If I had been told, while mixing ingredients in my Sunbeam mixer, that I would also be building an orphanage in Ukraine, I would not have believed them. But what I have learned along the way is that nothing is impossible with God. I did not have a burning desire to help the children in Ukraine until God placed these deserving people in my path and introduced me to their needs. Because my heart was open to hearing God's words, He was able to use me to help others. Never believe that where you are right now is where you will stay. Pray, have faith, and try to be of service to others. There are opportunities every day to help with hunger. Whether you donate to your local food bank or to your church, your generosity is desperately needed. A recent study shows that some 38 million people in America are considered "food insecure" by the government, and that number is growing. A portion of the proceeds from this cookbook will go to the Barnes Family Foundation, which will continue my mission to feed the hungry.

I am truly thankful for my family, my business, and my charitable organizations, and for all the wonderful friends in my life. I cannot imagine where else God will take me, but I will keep a watchful eye and an open heart toward the Lord. Bake bread, share, be kind to others, and thank God for your gifts!

May God bless you and keep you, always.

Sister Schubert

"No eye has seen, no ear has heard, no mind has conceived what God has prepared for those who love him."

—1 Corinthians 2:9

INDEX

A
Almond Christmas Braid 160
Angel Biscuits 87
Angel Corn Sticks 86
Applesauce Bread 97
Applesauce Muffins 80
Appletini, The Best 135
Artichoke and Ham Bruschetta 58
Artichoke Crab Dip, Sister's 120
Asparagus, Parmesan-Roasted 119
Aunt Charlotte's Quiche Lorraine 48
Aunt Mary's Coconut Pie 132
Avocado Salad, Grapefruit and, with Poppy Seed Dressing 51

B
Bacon, Maple, Steel-Cut Irish Oatmeal with 56
Bacon Marinara Sauce, Turkey Stuffed Shells with 147
Baking with Yeast 24
Banana Bread, Gommey's 96
Barbecue Sauce, Sister's, with Grilled Pork Tenderloin 68
Barbecued Brisket, Easy 72
Beef Tenderloin Rolls, Sister's 46
Bellini 136
Beverages:
    Bellini 136
    Best Appletini, The 135
    Classic Bloody Mary 135
    Classic Southern Mimosa 136
    Sister's Coffee Punch 137
Bishop's Brown Irish Soda Bread, The 112
Blueberry Muffins, Lemon- 83
Bread:
    Applesauce 97
    Banana, Gommey's 96
    Biscuits 87–89
    Breadsticks 84
    Buns, Hot Cross 152
    Buns, Sister's Sticky 53
    Challah 110
    Cherry-Cheese 100
    Christmas Braid 160
    Communion 113
    Corn Sticks 86
    Cornbreads 76–77
    Country 93
    Cranberry 141
    Easter 154
    Focaccia 102
    French, Classic 90
    Irish Soda, The Bishop's Brown 112
    Lemon-Poppy Seed 95
    Muffins 78–83
    Peach Crunch 98
    Pecan 92
    Scones 101
    Sourdough 104–106
    Tipsy Eggnog 153
    Wafers, Ukrainian Communion 114
Bread Of Life, The 108
Bread Pudding, Sister's Cinnamon 156
Breads 74
Breadsticks with Sister's Spicy Seasoning Salt 84
Breakfast & Brunch 38
Brisket, Easy Barbecued 72
Broccoli Cornbread 77
Brown Sugar Spread for Ham Sandwiches 145
Bruschetta, Artichoke and Ham 58
Buttermilk Biscuits 89
Butters:
    Herb Butter 37
    Honey Butter 37
    Maytag Blue Cheese Butter 37

C
Casserole, Sausage Roll Breakfast 52
Challah 110
Cheddar Rolls 33
Cheese Straws, Mama's 125
Cheesy Shrimp and Grits 49
Cherry-Cheese Bread 100
Chicken:
    Chicken and Sausage Gumbo 70
    Chicken Divan Crepes 42
    Chicken Velvet Soup 69

Grape Chicken Salad Canapés 57
Perfect Fried Chicken 65
Chili, George's 66
Christmas Braid, Almond 160
Christmas Sugar Cookies 157
Cinnamon Rolls 32
Classic Bloody Mary 135
Classic Southern Mimosa 136
Coconut Pie, Aunt Mary's 132
Coffee Cake, Easy 60
Coffee Punch, Sister's 137
Coleslaw, Sister's Fancy 124
Communion Bread 113
Corn Fritters, Fresh 118
Corn Sticks, Angel 86
Cornbread, Sister's Southern 76
Cornbread Dressing, Mamie's 150
Country Bread 93
Country Corn Muffins 78
Crab Dip, Sister's Artichoke 120
Cranberry Bread 141
Cranberry Conserve 140
Crepes:
    Crepe Batter 40
    Crepes, Chicken Divan 42
    Crepes, Lemon Dream 41
    Crepes, Smoked Salmon 44
    Crepes, Strawberries and Cream 45
Crepes 4 Ways 40
Crostini, Garlic Shrimp 61
Custard Fondue with Toasted Pound Cake 131

D

Desserts:
    Aunt Mary's Coconut Pie 132
    Christmas Sugar Cookies 157
    Cranberry Conserve 140
    Custard Fondue with Toasted Pound Cake 131
    Great-Grandmother Tee's Fudge Sauce 129
    Holiday Strudel 158
    King Cake for Mardi Gras 148
    Lemon-Blueberry Trifle 133

    Mama's Rum Sauce for Pound Cake 130
    Mama's Whipped Cream Pound Cake 128
    Pumpkin Mousse 146
    Sister's Cinnamon Bread Pudding 156
    White Chocolate Banana Roll Pudding 134
DESSERTS & BEVERAGES 126
Dip, Sister's Artichoke Crab 120
Dressing, Mamie's Cornbread 150
Dressing, Poppy Seed, Grapefruit and Avocado Salad with 51

E

Easter Bread 154
Easy Barbecued Brisket 72
Easy Coffee Cake 60
Everlasting Rolls 26–29

F

Family Favorites:
    Almond Christmas Braid 160
    Aunt Charlotte's Quiche Lorraine 48
    Breadsticks with Sister's Spicy Seasoning Salt 84
    Chicken Divan Crepes 42
    Chicken Velvet Soup 69
    Cheesy Shrimp and Grits 49
    Custard Fondue with Toasted Pound Cake 131
    Easy Coffee Cake 60
    Fly-off-the-Plate Pancakes 54
    Gommey's Banana Bread 96
    Great-Grandmother Tee's Fudge Sauce 129
    Grilled Pork Tenderloin with Sister's Barbecue Sauce 68
    Lemon Dream Crepes 41
    Lemon-Blueberry Muffins 83
    Mama's Rum Sauce for Pound Cake 130
    Mama's Whipped Cream Pound Cake 128
    Mamie's Potato Salad 122
    Raisin Sauce for Spiral-Sliced Ham 145
    Sausage Roll Breakfast Casserole 52
    Sister's Artichoke Crab Dip 120
    Sister's Beef Tenderloin Rolls 46
    Sister's Cinnamon Bread Pudding 156
    Sister's Southern Cornbread 76
    Sister's Tomato Pie 123
    Sweet Potatoes "Breard" 142

Fly-off-the-Plate Pancakes 54
Focaccia 102
Fondue, Custard, with Toasted Pound Cake 131
French Bread, Classic 90
Fresh Corn Fritters 118
Fried Chicken, Perfect 65
Fudge Sauce, Great-Grandmother Tee's 129

G
Garlic Shrimp Crostini 61
Gazpacho Shots with Mini Cornbread Muffins 50
George's Chili 66
Gommey's Banana Bread 96
Grape Chicken Salad Canapés 57
Grapefruit and Avocado Salad with Poppy Seed Dressing 51
Great-Grandmother Tee's Fudge Sauce 129
Grilled Pork Tenderloin with Sister's Barbecue Sauce 68
Grits, Cheesy Shrimp and 49
Gumbo, Chicken and Sausage 70

H
Ham Bruschetta, Artichoke and 58
Ham Sandwiches, Brown Sugar Spread for 145
Herb Butter 37
HOLIDAY FAVORITES 138
Holiday Strudel 158
HOMEMADE ROLLS 22
Honey Butter 37
Hot Cross Buns 152

K
King Cake for Mardi Gras 148

L
Lamb, Roasted Stuffed Leg of, with Shallot Sauce 64
Lemon:
    Lemon Dream Crepes 41
    Lemon-Blueberry Muffins 83
    Lemon-Blueberry Trifle 133
    Lemon-Poppy Seed Bread 95

M
MAIN DISHES 62
Mama's Cheese Straws 125
Mama's Rum Sauce for Pound Cake 130
Mama's Sourdough Bread 105
Mama's Whipped Cream Pound Cake 128
Mamie's Cornbread Dressing 150
Mamie's Everyday Biscuits 88
Mamie's Potato Salad 122
Maytag Blue Cheese Butter 37
Melon Mélange 46
Mousse, Pumpkin 146
Muffins, Lemon-Blueberry 83
Muffins Tropicale 81

O
Oatmeal, Steel-Cut Irish, with Maple Bacon 56
Orange Rolls 31

P
Pancakes, Fly-off-the-Plate 54
Parmesan-Roasted Asparagus 119
Peach Crunch Tea Bread 98
Pecan Bread 92
Perfect Fried Chicken 65
Po'Boys, Shrimp, with White Remoulade Sauce 73
Pork Tenderloin, Grilled, with Sister's Barbecue Sauce 68
Potato Salad, Mamie's 122
Pound Cake:
    Custard Fondue with Toasted Pound Cake 131
    Mama's Rum Sauce for Pound Cake 130
    Mama's Whipped Cream Pound Cake 128
Pudding, Bread, Sister's Cinnamon 156
Pumpkin Mousse 146
Punch, Sister's Coffee 137

Q
Quiche Lorraine, Aunt Charlotte's 48

R
Raisin Sauce for Spiral-Sliced Ham 145
Roasted Stuffed Leg of Lamb with Shallot Sauce 64
Roasted Vegetable Sandwiches with Herb Garlic Rolls 59
Rolls:
    Bites, Toasted 36
    Everlasting Rolls 26–29
    Herb Garlic 59
    Mediterranean 34
    Orange 31

Sausage 33
Sourdough 106
Turkey 34
Rum Sauce for Pound Cake, Mama's 130

S
Salmon Crepes, Smoked 44
Sauce:
    Great-Grandmother Tee's Fudge Sauce 129
    Mama's Rum Sauce for Pound Cake 130
    Raisin Sauce for Spiral-Sliced Ham 145
    Shallot Sauce, Roasted Stuffed Leg of Lamb with 64
    Sister's Barbecue Sauce, Grilled Pork Tenderloin with 68
    White Remoulade Sauce, Shrimp Po'Boys with 73
Sausage:
    Sausage Gumbo, Chicken and 70
    Sausage Roll Breakfast Casserole 52
    Sausage Rolls 33
Scones, Sister's 101
Shrimp:
    Shrimp and Grits, Cheesy 49
    Shrimp Crostini, Garlic 61
    Shrimp Po'Boys with White Remoulade Sauce 73
Sides & Veggies 116
Sister's Artichoke Crab Dip 120
Sister's Beef Tenderloin Rolls 46
Sister's Cinnamon Bread Pudding 156
Sister's Coffee Punch 137
Sister's Fancy Coleslaw 124
Sister's Scones 101
Sister's Southern Cornbread 76
Sister's Sticky Buns 53
Sister's Tomato Pie 123
Smoked Salmon Crepes 44
Soup, Chicken Velvet 69
Sourdough:
    Sourdough Bread, Mama's 105
    Sourdough Dos and Don'ts 104
    Sourdough Rolls 106
    Sourdough Starter 104
Steel-Cut Irish Oatmeal with Maple Bacon 56
Strawberries and Cream Crepes 45
Strudel, Holiday 158

Sweet Potato Pie 143
Sweet Potatoes "Breard" 142

T
Tipsy Eggnog Bread 153
Toasted Roll Bites 36
Tomato Pie, Sister's 123
Tomatoes Provençal 47
Turkey Rolls 34
Turkey Stuffed Shells with Bacon Marinara Sauce 147

U
Ukrainian Communion Wafers 114

V
Veggies, Sides & 116

W
White Chocolate Banana Roll Pudding 134
Whole Wheat *Everlasting Rolls* 29

Y
Yeast, Baking with 24

PHOTOGRAPH CREDITS:

Robert Evers: 165 (bottom right)

John Hollerand: 169

Leon Loard (with painting by Shari Ford): 172

Paul Poplis (with food styling by Sharon Reiss): 2, 6, 15, 22, 24, 25, 26, 28, 29, 30, 35, 38, 41(left), 43, 44, 48, 55, 58, 67, 71, 74, 76, 79, 81, 82, 85, 86, 89, 91, 92, 94, 99, 100, 103, 107, 108, 111, 115, 126, 129, 133, 138, 144, 148, 151, 153, 155, 159, 173 (left), 174

Vickie Popwell: 161, 165 (left and top right)

Romona Robbins: 170–171

Jessie Shepard: 20–21, 36 (left), 41 (right), 77 (right), 162–163, 168 (left), 173 (right)

2 cups sweet milk

½ recipe

Everlasting Rolls (Hollands)
1 qt sweet milk — 1 cup lard — 1 cup
sugar — Bring to the boiling point —
remove from fire & pour over 1 cake yeast
arm. Dissolved — Stir in 1 cake yeast
Stir in enough flour to make
a heavy batter of cake batter — about
a heaping quart.
Put in warm place 2 hours.
Then sift in 1 tblsp soda — 1 heaping
teasp baking powder — 1 heaping
teasp salt — flour enough
to make a medium stiff
shape or cut as many rolls as thought
if you wish — place in meal — let
as many before baking — rise for
2 hours before baking, generators
as much dough